CW01551774

To Lynne and Ronald Adams and family of Coventry UK for their kind encouragement, support, help and sustained interest given over a period of more than five years enabling me to develop a whole gamut of new possibilities. They have my most grateful thanks and appreciation.

Book Publishing Experience
(a beginners nightmare)

by Charles Round
C.Eng. FIME

©Copyright CR Publications 1999
ISBN 0953544109

Published by
CR Promotions
PO Box 467, Taunton TA1 5YX, Somerset

Typeset by Artytype, Lydney
Printed by APB Process Print, Bristol

Mr Charles Round
10 Lavender Grove
Biships Hull
Taunton

5 May 1999   From Tony Benn

Dear Mr Round,

Thank you very much for sending me a copy of your book describing your experiences as an author in getting your works published.

For anyone in the same position, it is a very interesting text book and the fact that we need to have publishing at the expense of authors is an indication of the failure of the publishing trade to serve its readership by making available a wide enough range of experience and opinion.

The right to free speech without the right to be heard applies in the printed word as well as public meetings which can be - and regularly are - completely ignored by the mass media.

Your own experience and efforts to bring this all into the public domaine represents a really important contribution.

I return the book with very best wishes.

With best wishes,

Tony Benn

CONTENTS

INTRODUCTION

Maybe you would like to write a book and have it published, a thought that must have occurred to many, many people. Fine – it's a creative and praiseworthy ambition, and one which has been accomplished by countless thousands of your fellow humans throughout the world.

If it is an adventure you are about to undertake for the first time, then I am sure you are really going to find it quite an experience. It can be in turn stimulating, exasperating, mortifying, emotional, costly, time consuming, worrying and hard work. If, however, you are gifted enough to be able to take such an enterprise readily and easily in your stride, you are indeed fortunate. May you exploit such talents to the full!

However, it is more than highly probable that, like me, you will be entering what becomes more and more evident – an uncharted minefield, calling for expert guidance, exacting enterprise, and determination. Problems and difficulties will arise which, from time to time, will lead you to question your initial judgement. Indeed, the experience can become quite traumatic and stressful.

However, once you have the bug and your idea simply refuses to become submerged in the nether regions of your mind, you have to take up the challenge, and doggedly deal with problems and difficulties as they confront your creative efforts blind to what lies ahead.

Although I had written technical papers, investigative and managerial and other reports, covering wide fields of activity, writing something for consumption in the 'public domain' never at any time entered my mind until, with advancing years, an unexpected stimulus created an uncontrollable impulse – regardless of potential cost, I was going to write and publish a book.

WHAT TO WRITE ABOUT?

First, of course, you have to have your subject. I believe there is hardly a single soul on this planet who doesn't, given the right circumstances, support and opportunity, have something to convey which is of concern and interest to someone else.

Written works cover all fields of thought – academic, scientific mathematical, religious, biographical, literary or technical.

The particular subject you choose for your initial adventure into the writing and publishing fields could be stimulated by experience, perhaps, in specialised fields such as politics, science and technology, commerce, industry, or history. Or perhaps you admire somebody who you would like to write a biography about. If you consider your own life interesting (or if others do) you might attempt an autobiography. Or perhaps you simply want to tell stories.

The motive for writing and publishing a manuscript is quite another matter. Financial gain, personal accolade, the desire to communicate one's experience to others, an attempt to influence social, legal, political or other situations come to mind, and there must be more..

Maybe financial gain is foremost? Unless we are well-known politicians, stars of stage and screen, sports personalities and anyone else strongly exposed to the public gaze in the process of doing either good or bad things, we cannot automatically be sure of high earnings from our writing.

Some of these people often do make great wealth from committing their experiences of office and other activities to open public gaze as written works, even if it is their first venture into this form of expression.

To ordinary people with a tale to tell or information to impart, the problem of not being an established writer is seriously retarding – despite the fact that most successful authors had to make a first effort.

Getting a mainstream publisher to accept work from an unknown author is an uphill struggle. We may not like the situation or even feel it is unfair, but we cannot change it.

Continual rejections can prove disheartening. But there is another route open to the would-be published author, albeit costly to the writer in terms of both risk and expense – the so-called "Vanity Press".

This is the route I chose to follow with my first book, and I hope that this account of my experience will serve as a guide – and perhaps a caution – to anyone considering the same path.

THE VANITY PRESS
The Vanity Press is a form of publishing in which a manuscript is edited, produced and promoted for an author under an agreed contract of terms and conditions. The bottom line is that the author pays for this process.

This form of publishing has attracted considerable criticism. It has been accused of questionable practices, including exploitation. Not all such publishers are guilty of nefarious practices but where these do arise they are often encouraged by human vanity transcending common sense. Excesses include financial rip-offs in the form of disproportionate capital charges, shortfalls in the agreed print run, overpricing of books in relation to potential sales, failures to meet deadlines in processing a manuscript and failures to promote the finished work. From time to time these transgressions are exposed in the national media.

The term "Subsidised Press" is really a variation on the Vanity Press theme. Both are cleverly promoted. Both make promises which are often not fulfilled.

Here are some points to watch out for:

1. A vanity (or subsidised) publisher will sometimes claim copyright for the work if the author unwittingly signs it away.
2. Authors who have paid for an entire press run actually receive only a fraction of the agreed run, and must purchase additional copies from the publisher.
3. Sometimes an author will be promised royalty, based on a percentage, after a certain number of copies are sold – rarely is that the case.
4. The publisher offers (at a cost) to list a book in its catalogue or to send out press releases for publicity. The catalogues typically do not generate many, if any, sales.
5. In some instances authors are asked to agree that contract disputes will be settled by arbitration rather than law.
6. Disclaimers provide for production and promotional delays and failures. with no adequate explanation.
8. Contract default production dates appear to have little meaning. The publisher covers himself with an author's signature of acceptance in situations of deadline default.

I have no doubt other pitfalls will be discovered.

The vanity publisher is not to be confused with a 'Book Packager'. The book packager is an expert who works for a fee, and does not usurp the author's legitimate rights connected with his or her book. Generally the packager will work as the author's contractor, process and build his or her book, obtaining all imprint credentials, International Standard Book Numbering (ISBN), bar codes and so on on behalf of the client.

The book will be carefully designed and credited to the author. Involvement of the author in all decision making processes, such as book size, design of covers, editing, print run, retail price and completed format, ensures the finished product more readily accords with the desire to end up with a well finished high quality product, giving the writer great satisfaction.

Some packaging companies specialise in book packaging. Others are independent publishers, while others are printers.

Turning back to the vanity press. Now, although a publishers' voluntary code of practice is in being which is designed to control misleading and untrue statements, dishonesty and unsupportable claims, it is considered to be ineffective, inept and inoperable. Lacking the weight of enforceable statutes, it has no repercussionary powers to exercise restraint on those publishers determined to act nefariously in pursuit of their own gains at the expense of the author and, indirectly, the public.

While commercial publishers would take on a book if they were certain that the entire economic print run would be sold, the criterion applied by vanity and subsidised press publishers is that only the author believes there is enough demand to make production a profitable venture.

But let's get back to authorship and the start of my story. How you are to get started is something of a personal nature. Stimulation from within is a matter of conviction that you have something to say and can make it attractive enough to warrant somebody else's interest. External stimulation on the other hand, may arise from the encouragement of other people that you have something worth the writing.

It was the latter which prompted the start of my personal adventure into writing.

In mid-October, 1993, my son John and his wife, Sue, invited me to join them on a 14 day holiday on Sanibel Island in Florida. I was to fly from Birmingham to New York and on to Atlanta. During the outward flight to New York I found myself sitting by an American-born lady, Mrs Lynn Adams, a Coventry school teacher married to Ron Adams, an English mathematician. She had been resident in the U.K. some 25 years or more. We started a discussion.

She asked me why was I making the trip, adding: "Have you been to America before?"

I told her about my trip and the fact I had visited the United States some five or six times previously.

She then asked: "Have you ever visited Pennsylvania? Do you know of a place called Barnsboro?"

This was fascinating. Yes I had a friends there - Richard (Dick) Todhunter, former president of the Barnes and Tucker Coal Company, and his two sons, Richard Jr and John. The former had served a term as mayor of the town.

Lynn told me her father, known as Gabby Roberts, had been treasurer for the Barnes and Tucker Coal Company and every Christmas Dick gave her and her sister presents, usually dolls.

Lynn was on her way to visit her aged mother (then in her early 90s) living very happily in a senior citizens' residential home in Philadelphia.

From that point she and I talked eagerly, and I told her of my experiences in the USA and as a mining engineer in the UK Coal Mining Industry covering well over 70 years. The seven-hour flight passed all too quickly. When we parted in Kennedy Airport she said: "All that you have told me Charles – is it written up, or recorded or on tape?"

I replied: "No – who would be interested?"

She said:"I found what you told me greatly absorbing."

I gave no further thought to the matter and continued my journey, and had a restful and enjoyable vacation with John and Sue.

On my return flight from Kennedy Airport to Birmingham, Lynn was again on my plane. Naturally we got together and our discussions followed on where we had left off

"I told Mother (Mrs Weltha Roberts) of our discussions on the way over and this gave her great pleasure," Lynn told me. "When I told her about Richard Todhunter, she walked to a cupboard from which she took a box of photographs. They had been taken many years ago when her mother was quite young. They showed her with with her husband, Gabby Roberts, together with the Todhunters during a joint underground inspection at one of their coal mines."

When we parted at Birmingham Lynn suggested that I wrote up my experience as a source of family reference.

Then she said: "Better still, publish them in a book and let me have copy."

She spoke with with such strong conviction that I was inspired. Later she sent copies of the photographs referred to, one of which features in the book I eventually published.

With the idea of acting upon her recommendation firmly fixed in my mind, and oblivious to what was to likely to follow, I worked on a manuscript for some two years. This was to involve some five draft preparations before I finally had one I was happy with, but I worked with a light heart.

I called my manuscript "Machinations in Coal Mining". It covers a very long and fruitful experience in the U.K. Coal Industry, over a period which was undoubtedly its most innovative and exciting episode, to which I had a dearth of "hands on" records relating – however, but for the incident of fate which led to my book, I would never have contemplated such a venture.

Let me outline some measure of the material that was available to me. It also serves to show how the basic material was chosen and later developed. It describes part of a book's evolutionary process and I hope it helps somebody not unlike myself at that time – a "would-be writer" completely inexperienced in authorship and publishing.

By outlining the experiences encountered along the way during those earlier creative efforts, it is my fervent hope that it will help the reader to deal with the pitfalls likely to be encountered if they are contemplating a similar venture.

At the same time, you may gain some interesting insights into the coal industry!

MY SYNOPSIS–FIRST MANUSCRIPT

Over the past 60 years or so, mining coal in the United Kingdom has been subjected to intense political, organisational and technical change, particularly so in the past 25 years.

On January 1, 1947, the number of operating collieries was of the order of 1,000. By 1994 fewer than 55 collieries were operative, a situation of decimation by any standards. Yet in terms of productivity, by employing the latest mining longwall technology the industry delivers some 50,000,000 tonnes per annum – more than half the output achieved when 1,000 mines were operating.

Since natural and unnatural selection over the past 37 years has played a great part in eliminating the non-viable (in the true sense of the term) exhausted collieries, it is reasonable to assume what we have left are those with the greatest potential.

The current mechanised space-age longwall mining systems have a degree of technical efficiency unmatched by any other contemporary underground mining systems anywhere in the world.

The 2 to 3 million tonnes-per-annum colliery is norm, and has a reliability factor of over 90 per cent. The mechanised longwall mining system" has been the subject of intense development over about 40 years, and its performance levels now are way beyond any other alternative system so far as deep mine production is concerned.

In simple terms, hand-worked machine longwall units formerly produced some 3,000 tons per week, later superseded by totally mechanised power loaded faces with which in the early 1960s reached 5,000 tons per week, with a reliability factor of probably 60 to 70 per cent (taking into account all aspects of breakdown, delay etc.).

From those early efforts of coal face and infrastructure mechanisation the modern longwall mechanised unit evolved embracing all the advances made over some 40 years. The mining system, design, planning, organisation and matching infrastructure elements of the system, in the form of production machines, powered supports, coalface conveyors, and underground transport have all come together in such a way that the weekly outputs from a mechanised single coalface unit now range between 50,000 and more than 250,000 tons a week in the most up-to-date situations.

Basically, the cause of the Coal Industry's comparatively rapid decline, (the ultimate effect of which could condemn future generations to the status of 'third world' citizens), was political. The Coal Industry was sacrificed on the altars of deceit, manipulation, political power, greed and party political interests. Successive government ministers and National Union of Mineworkers leaders must, I believe, jointly share the blame, in that the policy adopted by both sides was that whoever exerted the greatest pressure was king, rather than letting the Industry develop unfettered the vast economic potential of the immense coal reserves we are fortunate to have.

I have been actively and closely associated with the coal mining industry for upwards of 66 years and during my active life I took a leading role, along with many others, in the industry's technical development, raising its endeavours to high technical sophisticated achievements underground. Much arduous work has been eliminated and safety standards greatly enhanced to the high levels of those which prevail on the modern factory shop floor.

Against the experiences of a lifetime in the industry there is the background human story of my life, and how various events affected me and my family.

It is the story of a man starting out as a humble underground pony-driver at the age of 14, progressing through a wide range of other working activities to become a coalface worker, undertaking evening classes and technical college studies during which he subsequently obtained the basic mining qualifications for higher endeavours at a very early age.

Studying was somewhat second nature to his work and interests. Being endowed with a natural enthusiasm, considerable enjoyment was obtained from his efforts. These led him on to the work of an underground junior official then further into colliery management positions and later the highest area and national managerial appointments in the industry.

I included in my narrative the facts on three major mining disasters – the Sutton Colliery Explosion, Silverwood Colliery underground locomotive manriding fatalities, and the Aberfan Tip Disaster, the latter having a spill-over effect to an American Mine Disaster of a similar nature when I was subpoenaed to give details of my experience to American lawyers.

I also experienced two shaft winding incidents – the first an overwind at Gedling Colliery involving substantial damage to the surface headframe and shaft bottom winding structures, and the second at Clifton Colliery (also in the Nottingham Area) in which major damage destroyed one of the winding engine's steam cylinders during normal winding operations.

I was caught up in the business of local social welfare activities and old age pensioner associations particularly in the South Western Division. I spent time with Lady Megan Lloyd-George, cabinet minister Lord Halifax and Sir Grismond Phillips, Lord Lieutenant of Camarthenshire

I had personal interests in the brass band movement (both in South Yorkshire and West Wales) together with ventures into music recording. All are featured in the chronicle. Brass and vocal concerts in the Brangwyn Hall, Swansea, West Wales, and reference some 25 tape recorded band programmes also feature.

I took premature retirement, the circumstances of which are explained, and became a mining consultant working in connection with litigation and mining subsidence damage claims – the former with particular reference to American and Canadian mining companies – Kaiser Steel & MacDonald Porcupine Ltd respectively, in connection claims of more than $11 million.

The problems of human relationships and internal political pressures are not neglected, being dealt with in the direct manner of the Yorkshireman, without rancour, animosity or ill feeling.

With this huge amount of industrial and personal material to hand I shaped my first manuscript "Machinations in Coal Mining".

The next stage was getting it published.

A JOURNEY INTO PUBLISHING

Authorship Book No.2. - 14th October 1996

A NOVICE IN THE FIELD OF BOOK PUBLISHING
(BOOK PUBLISHING EXPERIENCE)

Structural Considerations

A S with any exploration into the unknown, determination is obviously a necessity without which we wouldn't travel very far. The first and most relevant question that can be asked is how we should prepare ourselves, starting with the supplies and equipment we might need.

FACILITIES AND AIDS

What did I have or need which would be helpful and reduce my effort? An early step was to obtain a copy of The Writer's Handbook (Published by Pan Macmillan Ltd) which proved helpful in many ways. It contributed to mapping out the proposed journey and provided detail of U.K, Irish. European and U.S. publishers and agents, with details of news agencies, regional newspapers, magazines and broadcasting companies and a wealth of other widely relevant and useful detail.

Obviously I needed some way of recording my experiences, ideas and thoughts and a way to store information for later manipulation. Primitive simple pencils, pens and paper and the old typewriter and its up-dated electronic counterparts have some limitations and today the personal computer, with it's versatility, speed, graphics and ease of editing, offers greater appeal.

COMPUTER HARDWARE

I GAVE up my old Olivetti Typewriter in the late 1980s and replaced it with a somewhat primitive IBM personal computer. It had a low-capacity hard disk and 4.5-inch floppy disks. Nevertheless I acquired a mild degree of competence with this equipment in the construction of reports for the consultancy work I had undertaken.at the time. But the set-up was limited, slow and frustrating, and lacked the ability to generate graphics. This led me to move on to an IBM-compatible Creative PC2 - CS computer, which had an 8x CD ROM, 16 megabytes of RAM, a 1 gigabyte hard disk, a modem, fax and a monochrome inkjet printer which I later updated to a colour version.

STRUCTURAL CONCEPTS

Before moving off it helps to decide upon landmarks. This is what I set down before attempting my second book, the one you are reading now.

1. Introduction – background circumstances leading to authorship in the first instance. Information – Brief account of initial entry into field of writing. Stimulus – to recount the experience of former efforts for the purpose.

2. Facilities and aids available. Personal computer – details of model and backup, hardware, computer programs, word processing. Spreadsheets and graphics, Microsoft Works .

3. Inspirational aspects – experiences of actual event during the course of editing earlier work, processing, and U.S.A comparisons. Imaginative and creative situations. Understanding more fully the publishing profession.

4. Manuscript development – main parts, sketching main sections. Headings, sub-headings and chapters. Research and development – choosing or rejecting material. Processing the manuscript – problems concerning a manscript's construction. Organisation of computer filing system. Revisions and re-drafts. Final acceptance.

5. Seeking a publisher. Direct approach to publisher. Alternative approaches.

6. Manuscript accepted. Contract considerations – United Kingdom and U.S experiences.

7. Processing manuscript using example of earlier work. Working with the publisher's staff – executive editor, manager, promotions co-ordinator, editorial director (ostensibly publisher). Problems and difficulties. Book published and enters public domain.

8. Promotion of book. Publisher's commitments – promotional strategy. Publishing campaign. Promotional responses – sales and revenue. Unsold copies.

9. General and specific conclusions .

10 Final analysis, comparisons. Was the effort worthwhile?

I suppose in simple terms this translates to getting one's thoughts down on paper, tape, computer or whatever at the earliest time one can.

PROCESSING THE FIRST MANUSCRIPT
The problems, difficulties and frustrations which developed during the publisher's processing of my first manuscript indicated to me that I had started the journey full of trust and complete faith – involving the

gentlemanly approach code I took as normal in former years.

In that disillusionment set in quite early. From the difficulties encountered it was quite apparent that written communication and follow-ups became more and more necessary in the pursuit of personal satisfaction. Although irksome and unfortunate, regretfully I found this to be necessary. In view of the charge of £14,000 which had been quoted it eventually became apparent to me (and indeed later to me and others) an excessive amount had been levied at the time.

Shortfalls in the publisher's organisational efficiency and achievements became obvious. With the tremendous experience I had covering 50 years or more in production and organisational activities, junior and senior, in the highest levels of colliery and area management. (and indeed national management) – I had quite a "yardstick" for comparative assessment. of relative performances which led repeatedly to calls for explanations.

Such an approach cannot be expected to endear one to his publisher. On one occasion I was informed my inquiries could bring about loss of respect among the publisher's staff. In another situation I faced apparent ridicule with adjectives such as "illogical" applied to the perfectly simple to understand situation of a senior citizen of well below average means watching every penny he spends with enforced care, and who on being offered the choice of buying the book through retail outlets at the price of £23.25 or $37.67 per copy, as opposed to the alternative through mail order at £25.25 or $41.0 per copy, finds it more economical to adopt the former approach.

To me both situations represent an attempted intellectual brush-off designed to discourage the author from pursuing what he feels to be his legitimate interests.

Maybe one or more repeated situations of this kind prompted the following statement from one publisher: "*Authors are easy enough to get on with - if you are fond of children*", (The Writer's Handbook, 1994 - Page 1).

I feel this indicates no small degree of implied contempt for the very people who have enabled, and have subsequently sustained the publisher in business since dawn of time and early cave inscriptions. I can't imagine the above to be a reflection of the general situation within the book-publishing industry. I am sure there are many publishers who still follow all that was traditionally the best in publisher/author public relationships.

Back to the work in hand. Having worked out the above structural arrangement and re-examined it at intervals during writing, I was prompted to ask two questions:

1. Am I attempting to write a simple treatise with the object of trying to advise the would-be first time author how to go about things " e.g. a somewhat formal approach?

2. Is it not better to treat the situation on a more informal basis, letting the reader work out his or her own thoughts, on the basis of seeing how one particular approach was undertaken, observing the mistakes made and

working out steps to circumvent any possible repetition of same within his or her own efforts?

One has to consider the possibilities of meeting the "good the bad and the ugly" (with acknowledgments to Clint Eastwood and the film industry) on similar terms, developing and adopting whatever measures are appropriate to each individual situation, and to seek professional advice where this felt to have become necessary.

I decided on the latter approach – firstly because, as a novice, one is in a learning stage. To attempt the role of a teacher with an assumed expertise I don't possess would be both presumptuous and out of character.

However there are situations in which an author has imaginative skills, within management, production, promotion, accountancy, and business situations generally, (together with other forms of experience) which can be highly contributory to a wide variety of different business disciplines and is able to give such support to the publisher in the conduct of their joint efforts in the processing, publishing and promotion of an author's. work.

Referring back to above structural format, the first variant has been the title change – with the object of trying simplify the nature of this second project.

GETTING STARTED
Getting together all the information and materials relative to the subjective account one wishes to write up, and assembling it in appropriate format and order, is a useful first step. Where the need arises for additional supporting material, e.g. illustration, statistics, verification, and the question of research, patience and restraint are called for. A determination to ensure ones confidence is not impaired by disappointment and frustration, which lurks in different guises within almost every avenue of endeavour, is most helpful.

Throughout my career, the basis upon which my first book, "Machinations in Coal Mining", was written, I had a squirrel-like approach to the collection of relevant mining information, new developments, operational financial and other reports, written-up ideas and innovations I was involved with, and of experience developed abroad particularly in the U.S., Germany and Spain. Unfortunately, with the passage of time and repeated changes of residence, much gets lost. However a sufficient volume of my former accumulations remained, which met my immediate needs and requirements. The structured arrangement made along the lines of the one shown for this current enterprise has proved most useful. Although time after time I found myself stranded by the next morning or after a good break, invariably I was able to continue my narrative often with the addition of supplementary but appropriate material not previously envisaged.

Thus I managed to proceed as the recall of past events readily came to mind. Picking up and examining a sketch, a plan, or a photograph without fail produced background memories of who was involved, and what was going on. With some 95 such illustrations readily available, the volume of recall was quite formidable and in many cases required strong decisions on whether or not particular incidents should be used.

The use of the PC, a formidable tool of resource, complexity and possibility, with a speed of execution and commitment way beyond my former and indeed current rate of achievement, was a great boon. However it threw up its own type of problems. In particular I had a steep learning curve to negotiate.

ASSEMBLING THE TEXT

As my working system I used GST-Pressworks alongside Microsoft Works for Windows Version 3.1.1, both incorporating word processing, spreadsheet and databank facilities. The former enabled me to meet the requirements of creating and manipulating text, and the spreadsheet helped me to construct and manipulate statistics in an executable mathematical format.

This latter facility really proved to be extremely useful in undertaking statistical research in connection with my travels. It is dealt with more fully later in the narrative. Databank provisions I did not use in those early stages but they have been useful for cataloguing audio cassettes, reel tapes, old 78 records and other recordings collected in great numbers over many years.

A great deal of wasted time, lost effort, wrongly directed travel, and frustration came my way during my first excursion into the field of book-publishing. Let me tell you of some of them. Maybe it will prove helpful to someone.

There is nothing more frustrating than to loose a full day's work embodying some 10 or 12 hours of arduous effort by a slip of the hand – unwittingly hitting the wrong key on the keyboard and erasing everything.

I experienced even greater calamities – the loss a great deal more than a day's work by careless erasure of material from both the hard or floppy disks. Lapses of concentration are lurking in the shadows of one's efforts, ready to disrupt or destroy creative effort. at all times. Such experiences prompted a degree of caution which produced difficulties of a different, yet potentially disastrous nature. Again, let me explain.

To offset the difficulties outlined in the foregoing paragraph I duplicated, and indeed even triplicated, copies of the same material under different file names, on different floppy disks. Therefore 'manus-1.wps', 'book-1.wps'. and ' machin-1", while they started off as the same material, quickly created havoc when I worked on this or that version. Identification of the most recently edited disk, added to corruption of the the basic material on other disks, gave rise to great difficulties.

Such was the cost of the zeal applied and anxiety expended at the peak of my mistaken endeavours, that I had more than 30 double sided high density (1,457, 667 bytes total disk space) floppy disks employed on the job – i.e. a total of 43,429,620 bytes. which in the final analysis was reduced to no more than 8,746,000 bytes.

Such an extravagant and incompetent approach, with its lapses of care and diminished confidence, arose from an emotional desire to push on with the work, often with an unwarranted degree of urgency (in my former career, often a good basic approach to getting things done on time) and to miss nothing that could be construed to be relevant.

Such an approach had its price. Confusion! Even at a late stage in one's life some things are still learned, regretfully ,the hard way. Although the impact is deeper and more intense, it is a costly way of achieving experience.

In the exercise of creating a manuscript, the American KISS concept (Keep It Simple Stupid) is worthy of the deepest consideration and application.

All programmes connected with the manuscript's production including chapters, illustrations and statistics, were transferred into an individual identified folder.

Correspondence with the publisher's staff – executive editor, publishing manager and promotions manager – were also transferred to a separate identified folder.

The directory chart which follows shows how it was undertaken. With this arrangement, relevant and common subjects can be kept together in a more systematic manner. Formerly, with my haphazard filing, much time was lost in trying to remember which floppy disk contained the file or information being sought and where it was located.

Good discipline in this direction leads to an orderly and more certain approach. Moreover, it reduces the chance of anxiety and carelessness leading to wasted effort.

SKETCHES AND PHOTOGRAPHS

Sketches were produced with the aid of a graphic software programme which, for the purposes I had in mind, did an excellent job, despite the fact it took me quite some time to settle in and to work with confidence. I really enjoy creating graphics on the computer, despite the fact that I have a great deal to learn both with regard to the process and execution. Maybe that arises because of the early training I received in engineering drawing at technical college many, many years ago. One feature of the Aldus programme is the facility to use coloured guides (invisible to printout operations) which I found helpful. Unfortunately due to space available, sketches in this final draft have been limited.

In the course of my former creative endeavours I came across the statement *"one picture is worth 1,000 words"*. I have no doubt but that this is so, particularly where technical or other specialised information and experience is being introduced to lay minds.

During my journey into the realms of publishing and would-be authorship, full use of this old aphorism was applied along the way. I had a copious amount of illustration in photographic, sketch, plan, chart and other graphical formats to draw upon, and as such made full use of my resources.

I have always been able to transform thought and ideas generally into this method of communication, or into engineering type sketches or drawings,

throughout my long technical and managerial career. This has proved helpful on countless occasions. In that first publishing adventure, with a total of 96 figures, photographs, plans and sketches, potentially at least 100,000 words have been saved.

At last I arrived at the end of this part of my journey with the final manuscript draft completed.

At that point I was satisfied with what been so painstakingly achieved, though one can never be totally gratified.

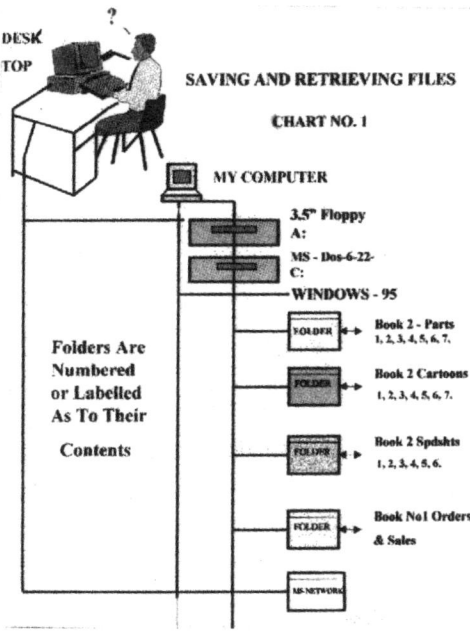

SAVING AND RETRIEVING FILES

CHART NO. 1

**WORKING WITH IBM COMPATIBLE COMPUTER
CHART NO.1 SAVING & RETRIEVING FILES**

1. Save build-up of Text & Sketches at frequent and short intervals.
2. Avoid heavy duplication of program or files – 1 hard disk and 1 floppy sufficient.
3. Save and Retrieve programmes and file systematically in appropriate folders.
4. Label folders, programs, files and floppy disks as to content to facilitate ease of saving discovery and recall.
5. Exercise great care in DELETION OF FILES AND PROGRAMS. Many hours of work were lost in that respect.

SEEKING A PUBLISHER

With my emotions fully charged and confident in the belief that I had really had produced a masterpiece the public had been waiting for, I set out to find a publisher. The strength of those emotions and convictions surprise me even today after a career of some 70 or more years associated with the U.K.coal mining industry.

After such a long time, in a business far removed from authorship it was quite amazing how much this affected me.

As a seasoned campaigner, having been subjected to elation, many successes, failures, frustration, disappointment and dirty tricks over many years, I cannot for the life of me understand what gave rise to the sensation. But so it was. It certainly wasn't the result of any prospect of material gain or belief that I would make very much money, for I had done what I had always done throughout my former career – become beset with an idea that had to be pursued with no relaxation of effort, and with no thought of financial outcomes. Further reflection on this situation satisfied me in the belief that I had still retained what was and is a fine characteristic, despite long exposure to many pressures – enthusiasm.

Not knowing how to move in this new direction I spent a considerable time in W.H.Smith's Taunton, Somerset branch one Monday morning, examining books of all kinds which I thought might help me on the subject of writing and publishing. Nothing seemed to fit the bill. As I tried to explain what I was after to the sales staff, the lady in charge turned to me and said: "What you want is a copy of Pan Macmillan's Writer's Handbook – I believe we have a 1994 copy in stock."

Off she went and after some five minutes returned with the only copy available. Thus I became further equipped to continue my journey.

I believe my timing was right in the purchase of this very useful book for would-be authors. Had I bought it earlier I might well have become preoccupied with a conventional approach to writing and publishing. Thus I may have produced something which would have been somewhat foreign to my nature, particularly as some of the best teaching in life is by learning the hard–way. It cuts deeper and sticks more firmly – not that I would always recommend such an approach. It exacts a heavy price in many situations.

The contents of this reference work quickly dispersed any thoughts I had of submitting my work in its format at that time. Such an approach would certainly have been doomed in view of the high number of rejections that can take place in mainstream publishing. American experience testifies to a constant barrage of unsolicited manuscript arriving by mail and indeed by fax – "over the transom" is the phrase they use. Because it is considered such manuscripts are generally of no merit they are directed into the "slush pile", a forbidding heap of cardboard boxes each counting a novel or some other work. Hardly one of these manuscripts ever appears as a published book, the system being well served with effective screening provisions. Well paid senior editors cannot be allowed to waste time on unpromising material.

Research indicates that only one manuscript in 900 of those received ever becomes a book, although there is always the exception in which a work with five or more rejections survives to become a "best seller".

CONTACTING PUBLISHERS

The possibility of first approaching an agent was felt to be premature at this early stage, in that I had not yet tested acceptance or rejection of the manuscript by a publisher. Maybe I was wrong – I don't know – but with hindsight I do feel there is merit in considering the services of an agent, especially when a manuscript has been accepted and a contract is soon to be signed,

Deciding upon a direct approach to a publisher rather than an indirect one, an agent, the list of U.K publishers was carefully foraged through. One stood out, being situated in Yorkshire and being part of Barnsley Chronicle Holdings, an old established publishing and printing house familiar to me during my boyhood and youth.

Trading was being undertaken as Wharncliffe Publishing Limited, 47 Church Street, Barnsley, South Yorkshire.

A letter was written to them on March 24 1994 and I received a response on April 7, 1994.

Wharncliffe Publishing publishes books of local interest to the Barnsley area and no doubt there is information in your book which is of great interest to us. However it is difficult to evaluate the book on the information you have supplied as there are no details of the various chapters, contained In the book. We would also find it helpful in making up our minds if we could see a sample chapter, preferable one covering your time in the Barnsley Area
– Managing Director.

The appropriate material suggested was sent to them on April 18, which evoked an acknowledgement and later a rejection on July 5.

We have produced a couple of books on coal mining, and one or two others which involved coal mining, therefore your book is of great interest to us. Also there is no doubt your book would be of interest to students of coal mining history, but from our point of view our publications are heavily oriented to the Barnsley area and your book

covers too much about the other areas. Regretfully I do not see ourselves publishing this book.
– Managing Director

Somewhat disappointed, I consulted the Writer's Handbook once again, and this time I was attracted to Judy Piatkus (Publishers) Ltd.

From the description of the publishing house in the handbook it looked a most attractive possibility. A letter was addressed to Judy Piatkus (Publishers) Ltd, 5 Windmill Street, London W1. with a synopsis and specimen chapters under the title "A Lifetime in Coal Mining" (my first choice of title).

A rejection note was received some time later.

Thank you for your synopsis and sample chapters. I do apologise for delay in replying – this was simply due to the sheer volume of manuscripts we have received. After careful consideration, I am afraid we felt that your proposed book was not right for our list at present. I am therefore returning your material.
Thank you again for letting me see your work and I hope you find a suitable publisher.
– Assistant to Judy Piatkus.

Although a little crushed, I subjected the manuscript to considerable scrutiny, following which I concluded that it fell short of the standards it could well have attained and that a great deal more effort had to be applied. From that point, with great determination, I wrote further drafts and continued so to do even after two more rejections.

At that point I felt I'd raised the final draft to a level which gave me satisfaction.

My next approach was to an agent, the outcome of which was a further rejection.

Throughout this aspect of the adventure one is subjected to heavy frustration and impatience.

Looking back, I benefited greatly from the rejections, all of which gave me a greater perspective of what was really involved and strengthened my determination to produce something I felt to be worthwhile.

Then, by chance, I became involved with the Carlton Press Corporation, New York.

The circumstances and the events arising from them are quite unique.

A long, long time before approaching both Wharncliffe Publishing Ltd and Piatkus Books as potentially interested parties, I had received out of the blue details of Carlton's activities as a publishing house in the form of a free copy of a work entitled How to Publish Your Book. This I had aside, for at the time I had neither the idea or intent of becoming involved in authorship.

Now, bouncing back from the disappointments described, I retrieved the information on Carlton in February 1995 and submitted a synopsis and sample

FRUSTRATION
Our Friend The Postman

Postman Pat became one of our most anticipated callers leaving us with no little disappointment when he failed to call.

Whilst 'Trash Mail' is around in greater quantities – and Insurance Companies, Banks & Finance Houses find greater urgency for me to invest monies I haven't got yet.

What makes Manuscript Acceptance & Book Orders to be so elusive?

Kim our family pet has got the mood and is now friendly to Pat.

of part of the manuscript to the firm's New York address, even though I was still not fully satisfied with my efforts (while many improvements had been made, I still felt I should continue to try to achieve higher standards).

I received a reply from Carlton on February 28 which included the following details.

Thank you for your letter which we have just received. It has aroused immediate interest here and we are now extremely eager to see the complete manuscript.

As no two books are alike, it is not possible to judge sight unseen (or even from sample pages) the style, overall quality, costs of publication, design format, artwork, typography, editorial hours, promotion and publicity are amongst the many factors which can only be determined after we have seen & evaluated your entire book. Will you therefore please forward your complete manuscript to us at your very earliest convenience? If this is not possible, please advise us as to approximately when you will send it so we can schedule it for a reading.

As soon as your completed manuscript is received, our professional reader's evaluation will be rushed to you at no charge or obligation. Any publishing agreement we can then offer you will clearly state all the vital benefits. and services to be provided by us for the one low amount specified and with no costs whatever

Under our subsidy publication program the Author receives a very liberal 60 per cent of all books sold.

– Executive Vice President.

The manuscript was sent forthwith following which on April 21, 1995, I was informed of the editing staff's assessment of my manuscript:

MACHINATIONS IN COAL-MINING is a fascinating combination of both autobiographical account and historical document merged into one insightful volume about the coal mining industry. Charles Round shares his firsthand knowledge and experience of the industry as he attempts to write in non–technical language. Here is a probing and enlightening investigation of an industry that many readers know nothing about and it will surely make for an educational experience. Even as we are thoroughly convinced of the author's intelligence, eloquence and perceptiveness, we are also impressed by the research and time that has been devoted to this insightful book. (Our editor will correct minor errors in spelling and punctuation along with some judicious pruning of subordinate detail. If you have in addition the manuscript available – text only – on computer disk, please send it along to facilitate the editing process.).

– Executive Vice President.

Receipt of this letter was a most uplifting experience. Moreover, it enlightened me as to other relevant aspects in the publishing trade, among them:

> We plan a format that will appeal to both booksellers and the public. We will create an attractive cover design, with harmonising binding, high quality printing on smooth offset paper with ample margins and an appealing typography. One of our editors will send a jacket copy and a biographical sketch for your review and approval. Illustrations will be printed monochromatically (unless otherwise stipulated in your contract) and our design department will immediately begin planning your jacket which again, will be sent to you for approval. (Your publicity questionnaire and a good black and white photo will assist us with our promotional activities.). We plan to publish your book under Carlton Hearthstone imprint. Beyond the editorial and production considerations, your book offers a variety of possibilities for promotion and publicity. Press releases will be sent to targeted radio and television stations, as well as a number of national or specialised magazines and newspapers. Copies of your book will be mailed to reviewers and booksellers and libraries and possible specialised outlets. We will attempt to arrange personal interviews and book signing receptions convenient to you and advertisement space will be reserved in local and regional newspapers. Where appropriate we will explore the subsidiary rights market – book-clubs, reprint houses, foreign rights, premium and other sales. Furthermore a description of your book will be included in the next edition of the Carlton Press Catalogue. and your title will be listed in such essential trade reference sources and BOOKS IN PRINT and TRADE LIST ANNUAL For the protection of you and your heirs, the copyright of your book will be interested in your name. As you know, no publisher can predict how well a book will sell. In fact the range might be anywhere from just a few copies to a very successful run. So much depends on the positive response of reviewers, and retailers finding a home for your book in a very competitive market place. In the subsidy programme success ultimately depends on the author and his or her work. In any case you can be assured that the editorial design, and production aspects clearly specified in the agreement will be fulfiled, so that you book will become an extremely attractive volume in which you and your family, friends and associates can take considerable pride.
> – Senior Vice President.

Accompanying this letter was the company's publishing agreement (to be dealt under contract considerations later) which I found highly informative, particularly with its treatment of the publicity and promotional aspects.

Naturally I was highly elated and stimulated. I signed the contract. I have no reservations, with hindsight, of having done this – but circumstances subsequently developed in a manner which created such a degree of nervousness I became most unsettled and uncertain.

In view of the distance to Carlton in America (which I felt might give rise to communication difficulties), I wrote to ask the senior vice–president for a fax number – there was none on their letterheadings.

The reply was yes, they had a fax number, but it was for company and not for general use.

"Why?" I enquired. The reply was:

"When it was freely issued we were being faxed with unsolicited manuscripts throughout each day disrupting our normal business and adding to our costs."

In accordance with the terms of the contract I submitted a banker's draft in the value of $18,700.00 (£12,100. approx) on May 1 1995, and by separate parcel post forwarded the manuscript, photographs and associated material to the address in New York.

Both were lost in transit for a number of weeks .

I consulted my bankers and my solicitor, Mr R.W. Hemmings of Taunton, who convinced me to cancel the contract since it had only my signature. This he undertook for me. Incidentally, he also read my manuscript to see if it contained inadvertent libels or other legal discrepancies, and he was most impressed and congratulatory about the work.

Carlton Press Incorporated responded with great disappointment. However, the implications involved in the possible loss of such a sizeable amount of work and money were to me highly disturbing, almost to point of total abandonment of the project. The publisher was as helpful as he could be within the confines of the situation and acted with the greatest of propriety and integrity in the circumstances. Both banker's draft and lost material were subsequently discovered and returned to me.

I now needed to find another publisher offering the same sort of service as Carlton. Examining the book reviews in a copy of Mining Technology journal, I came across a Publishing Firm. I made inquiries about their services and it was indicated they were able to supply what I was looking for. I sent a synopsis with detail of the manuscript to them on October 17, 1995.

By return of post I was requested by the executive editor to send her the complete manuscript for appraisal. In her letter she set out the background information regarding the way in which their publishing house operates. I can do no better than to reproduce the points:

We enjoy a publishing pedigree which is second to none. Our company is based upon good, old fashioned values which are tried and tested and long established. Concepts such as tradition, an unrivalled attention to detail and obsession with quality are the hallmarks of our organisation. If you add to these the sort of personal service which is almost impossible to find these days and amounts to cossetting our authors, then you may gain a flavour of the sort of philosophy which has our company so successful and which are proud to offer.

We can also offer a method of operating which we consider to be unique and very much to the advantage of authors. We work on the basis whereby the cost of publishing the first edition of a book is borne by the fees payable at key stages during the publishing process. The author then receives the entire revenue from the sales of all books in this first edition. It is always our aim that the authors more than recover their financial investments in the project from the sales of books in the first edition.

A second edition and any subsequent editions would then be produced entirely at our expense and, from sales of books in these editions, authors receive royalty payments of not less than 15 per cent which is generally accepted as a generous resulting revenue again being paid exclusively to the author. Perhaps this is why so many of our authors return to us for the service highly recommended by authors and associations alike. It is difficult to provide a firm indication of the precise scale of investment required for publication since there are a number of variable factors which can only be determined on the sight of the manuscript. As a guide, however, an author's contribution to the publication of a book would be at least £3,500, with an average probably being in the region of £6,000.

We would be disappointed however, if any investment made by the author, whatever the sum, was not recovered from the sales of the books in the first edition.

Throughout the whole publication process we provide a completely personal service to all of our authors, guiding and advising at each and every stage. We believe fundamentally in this individual treatment and high level of author commitment. That they are vital elements in our policy. is, in part, because no two books are alike – each book and author need to be handled with their own specific needs uppermost; it is also because we are very mindful of the financial investment and feel that the author's close interest in the publishing business is the best way of safeguarding his investment. To this end we have a team of editors, experienced in a wide range of genres, who work closely with authors to prepare manuscripts for printing, and excellent artists who produce sets of jacket designs from which authors can make a choice.

We also attend to all standard book numbering details and registration with copyright libraries. Equal attention is given to the area of promotion and marketing. We are acutely aware of the need to market books successfully and have a dedicated promotion team

who will prepare a full promotional schedule to market each book to the best possible advantage. Above all we are conscious of the time and effort which authors have devoted to their manuscripts and are extremely proud of the books we publish – inevitably of the highest quality.
– Executive Director.

Letters of this type, issued by one of the company's senior staff, must surely be regarded as an expression of company policy and read as if they apply to whatever contract terms are negotiated. It is not unreasonable for the would-be author to question in bona–fide situations, any lack of adherence to such statements, if it is felt personal matters of interest are not proceeding satisfactorily or promises are not being kept. To raise such matters of concern is in the interests of the publisher – by such means he is appraised of circumstances, staff failures and other situations likely to adversely affect the company's interests.

In view of the importance of a document of this kind, and in the light of what follows and is later outlined, it is worthy of analysis at this stage.

1. As a document of positive assurance to the would-be writer or first-time author, it has been extremely well prepared. Taken at its face value an author can be excused if he feels safe & secure. At this stage he has no measuring yardstick or knowledge with which to accept the situation in any other way.

2. It is quite a conditioning instrument in the sense that it is sent before any sighting of a potential contract. Emotionally boosted by his manuscript's acceptance for publication, is it reasonable to expect a first-time-writer to treat any potential contract" with the cold scrutiny of a legal mind? With the average person, I don't think so!

It is at this point that it is felt the publisher should appraise the author (with this particular type of contract in question). of the sort of disappointments and/or pitfalls likely to be encountered from time to time. After all, the publisher is the only one with the experience in such matters,

Let us examine in the light of events some of the points made in the letter, starting with the reference to the company's Raleigh, North Carolina Division. After publication, a number of American friends tried to get a copy of my book through this agency but were unable to do so. What significance does the U.S. address have other than simply trying to impress the would-be author?

The company also says it has grown to be the largest and most successful publishing company of its type in the United Kingdom.

On what grounds does that success and size exist:– financial turnover, number of books published, first edition sales, number of reprints, writer satisfaction, manuscripts submitted, rejection rate? How are the comparisons made?

A categorical statement is also made to the effect that "a publishing pedigree second to none" exists. On what and on whose judgements is that based?

Precisely what is the "personal service, amounting to cossetting of authors" in practice?

In what sense is the publisher's method of operation unique? Is it the only one of its kind, as the literal meaning of the adjective indicates?

In what manner, compared with other arrangements within the book publishing trade, is the "method of operating" very much to the advantage of an author.?

What percentage of the books published achieve the publisher's aim of recovering more than the author's financial investments, and over what period does this arise?.

It is true that an author makes full payment of the capital sum agreed before a book is made available to public exposure or promotion, and is it also true that the publisher, having received full payment, thereafter takes no further risk in the book's success or otherwise?

In such circumstances, can one expect a publisher, taking no risk, and having in the first edition stages no financial motivation in the success of an author's arduously developed, applied and self-funded efforts, to apply himself with the same degree of applied intensity in the promotion of the book, as would be the case where he had direct and personal financial interests invested therein? I think not.

How can it be that, with the publisher totally funding second and subsequent editions of his book, a minimum royalty payment, of not less than 15 per cent to the author, is regarded as generous, particularly in a situation where the success of the title has been obtained in spite of, rather than with the determined support of, the publisher's effort?

In the publisher's 1995 book list embracing some 150 primary and 184 secondary books, in the primary list one author (former creator of some 150 railway books) had two books published in the category of Memoirs/ Autobiographies. Another author in the category Philosophy had four books published, the first of which embraced two volumes. In the Other Titles secondary list, a third author had two books featured. I believe all three authors were satisfied within their particular circumstances. However, such lists cannot disclose or indicate those authors who sought to have their subsequent works or titles published elsewhere, which is a test of satisfaction.

Referring to the difficulties of providing a firm or precise indication of the scale of an author's investment required for the publication of his unseen manuscript – this must obviously be a price accepted as both fair and reasonable to both parties.

What is of real interest is the guide to the scale of that investment – at least £3,500 and a probable average price of £6,000, the highest value of the range to which these values apply is not quoted.

If these figures were to have any real meaning, they would obviously have been determined as a specific range of values in which the probable maximum author's capital investment could be quoted. However, to quote a probable maximum capital investment charge, subjects the publisher to the risk of being asked to account for any substantial departures therefrom. In the absence of the range of elemental values from which the quoted levels of lower and average charges were determined, and assuming an equal spread between the lower level, average level and upper level values, I do not think it unreasonable to interpolate the upper level of capital charge in the following way:

PUBLISHER 1'ST BOOK   **AUTHOR/PUBLISHER 2'ND BOOK**
CAPITAL – £14,000   **CAPITAL £5,000**
PRINT RUN – 800   **PRINT RUN – 1,500**
Price £17.50 Per Book (Actual) Price £3.33 Per Book (Actual)

PUBLISHER'S ROUGH GUIDE TO CAPITAL COSTS
MINIMUM – £3,500 – PROBABLE AVERAGE – £6,000

C | Upper Level of Series – £8,500 | Ceiling

$C - A = £8,500 - £6,000 = £2,500$ $C = \{£6,000 + (£6,000 - £3,500)\}$

A | Average Level of Series - £6,000 | Average

$A - B = £6,000 - £3,500 = £2,500$ $A = \{B + C\}/2 = (£8500 + £3,500)/2$
$= 12,000/2 = £6,000$

B | Lower Level of Series - £3,500 | Bottom

Interpolation of Capital Ceiling
Average & Lower Levels Values
Given as Indicated

In the event, my capital charge fixed at £14, 472 represents a very substantial departure over and above the figure just determined, (quite an extraordinary situation, irrespective of the factors involved).

One explanation lies in the belief there is no limit to escalating costs – quite a dangerous assumption, where such costs are passed on to the consumer without any effort being made by the publisher either to control or reduce them. In a highly competitive situation, he would find a limit had been reached when he went out of business.

Great emphasis is placed on the publisher's approach to publisher/author relationships. It is difficult to envisage how a situation of conflict or loss of confidence could arise between the two parties,with the sincere application of the concepts described.

Registration in copyright libraries is understood to be mandatory and embraces the libraries of Cambridge, Oxford and Trinity College Dublin.

It is both pertinent, proper and advisable to acknowledge in all fairness to the publisher, the following:

Publisher states:

> *As you know, no publisher can predict how well a book will sell. In fact the range might be anywhere from just a few copies to a very successful run. So much depends on the positive response of reviewers, and retailers finding a home for your book in a very competitive market place..*

However, how skillfully the book is promoted does have some influence on the public's reaction:

My own opinion is that:

> *If retail outlets are not informed of a book's existence, provided with exhibition copies, launching sessions, exhibitions with all the trimmings of modern advertising and promotion, together with a carefully thought out retail book price acceptable to the widest range of market potential, public reaction becomes dependent upon word–of–mouth projection in whatever form it takes, between members of the public, book clubs, authors' lectures,*

His statement endorses lack of effort on the part of the publisher or promoter. It presents a negative approach, in that things can be made to happen if the will is there on the part of the publisher to accomplish this. Whatever the shortfall I eventually experienced, I am sure it would certainly have been much worse had I not made great efforts.

In a situation where there has been a "lead time" of upwards of 12 months in relation to informing retail outlets of a title's advent, only to find upwards of three months still later that the U.K's leading book trade retail outlets express ignorance of the book's existence, how is an author expected to feel? I also had relatives, friends and members of the public tell me they could not find the book in the shops. To some I gave the address of the publisher to make a complaint.

One lady wrote a very constructive letter to them explaining the situation. The response was to the effect: that she should obtain a copy through mail order. (The Author will make more money for himself that way!)

Both she and I were incensed by what seemed to me such a cavalier approach – somewhat reminiscent of the "if you like children"statement referred to earlier.

Her response was quite direct: She wrote saying she had neither the desire, nor intent to needlessly pay £2 more for her purchase than was required – nor was she prepared to act as salesperson for either the publisher or the author.

She received no reply. It was several weeks before she obtained a copy through a local bookstore in Teeside.

The advice she had been given was quite perplexing and posed to me this problem: How does any member of the public obtain copy of an author's book, having failed to find one through a retail outlet, and without any information from the publisher or author of the existence of any mail order provisions?

PUBLIC RELATIONS OFFICER

This particular situation and others of a similar nature which later followed, with the irksome correspojndence generated, leading to a final breakdown of publisher/author relationships, suggest in the circumstance outlined hereto and hereafter there could be merit in the Publisher's appointment of a Skilled Public Relations Officer. Such an appointment could have great merit in a variety of ways – particularly with the ramifications and signing of publishing contracts.

ACCEPTANCE

Following the submission of my manuscript on October 17, 1996, I received a charming short letter from the publisher's executive editor which acknowledged its receipt. It included the following:

"... upon first glance [your manuscript] appears quite impressive. Your material will now be considered by one of our readers and, when we have discussed your work in detail, I will contact you with an appraisal and any proposals. – Executive Editor.

U.K PUBLISHER'S AND AUTHOR'S JOINT ACCEPTANCE
On November 9 I was informed of the publisher's willingness to accept the manuscript for publication in the following terms:

"We now have had the opportunity of appraising your manuscript, Machinations in Coal-mining, which proved as anticipated to be very impressive. I have received the reader's report which is most complimentary, a copy of which I enclose for your perusal, and have also discussed the project in some detail with our editorial department here .

"As you can see, the reader's report is most complimentary and one with which we are all in complete agreement. You have written an authoritative and informative account of your personal experience in the mining Industry. Machinations in Coal-mining is a work of tremendous scope which is, nevertheless, eminently readable and packed with a wealth of fascinating detail. It is also a work of historical significance. The coal industry is an integral part of Britain's heritage, not only in terms mechanised growth, but also in social and cultural terms: for many years the nature of the industry directly influenced the quality of people's lives and shaped the destiny of hundreds of communities for the greater part of the twentieth century. I feel that the importance of a book such as this cannot be underrated and will ensure its place as a valid and viable work of reference. However, you have a fascinating personal story to tell, and the account of your own professional achievements is an absorbing read in itself. Overall we feel that Machinations in Coal-mining is a very worthy and accomplished book which is likely to be well-received by a wide audience. As you have no doubt deduced from our

book list, we are selective in the material we include, primarily because we are only prepared to accept works which we consider to have a potential to be successful. Your book certainly falls into this category. I feel your work would enhance our lists considerably and would be pleased to undertake publication if you decide to proceed with this.
– Executive Editor

Turning my attention to the reader's report enclosed with the above letter, I really felt somewhat on top of the world, but what was to follow was way beyond anything I could have imagined Maybe you would like to judge for yourself?

READER'S REPORT – TITLE: Machinations in Coal-mining
AUTHOR: Charles Round
READER: Graham Almond.
DATE TO READER: October 25 1995.
This manuscript represents a phenomenal achievement. Machinations in Coal-mining is a huge book dealing with one man's rise through the ranks of the coal industry, from pit pony driver to the controller of several pits. On one level, this is a straightforward autobiography (we hear of Charles Round's family and interests), but it is also a pertinent and very valuable historical work, with features which impinge on the lives of many. The work incorporates a wealth of factual detail, and the reader is told of the mechanics and machines needed for modern mining; the National Coal Board, its successes and failures; and miners, at the coal-face, or in the boardroom.
Few features of the post-war coal industry can be missing; it seems that everything and everybody is here, from Aberfan to Arthur Scargill. This is not only a large book, it is intricate and complete. The author must be congratulated for the time and commitment he has given to this project, and congratulated for the quality of work. Whilst the narrative tells a story of birth, school, work and promotion, the photographs and diagrams give the work a broader scope. The diagrams are fascinating, with detailed computer line drawings explaining the intricate constructions of pit shafts, for example. The photographs are also wonderful, museum-worthy affairs, relating to the history of men underground, and frighteningly-complex cutting tools, which would take a million words to tell. Understandingly, I have a few favourite pictures, but will mention just one – No.66 shows a coal-encrusted miner with a powerful shearer – human effort and mechanised power, which sums up post-war mining. I expected Machinations in Coal-mining to be an illustrating book – the author spent his life in a rapidly evolving industry – however, I was pleasantly surprised to find that the style of

the book is altogether more noteworthy. The writing is lucid and involving, with a clear thread to the narrative, and time to remember other characters of the story, through conversations and telling descriptions. The organising is also exemplary – a chronological review, neatly divided into chapters and subheadings. There is even an index. The author was also never afraid to make full use of powerful modern software, utilising many different type-styles. Scientific correctness decreed that the post-war years were the halcyon days of scientific endeavour, culminating in cheap, inexhaustible atomic energy. We now know that nuclear power is fraudulently expensive, and will be potentially lethal for millennia to come. This book covers what should have been the golden age of coal mining. The author was heavily involved in the subterranean revolution, replacing men with shovels for fantastic mechanisation. With so many recent politically motivated pit closures, something is needed to preserve details of this progress forever. The Nuclear Age has its own monuments (Chernobyl for example); coal mining needs books such as Machinations in Coal-mining to keep its memory alive. Overall this is an exhaustive study of a fascinating subject. The book is an educational work as well as an historical document. I have no doubt that it is a viable work for publication."

What I found remarkable from the above assessment was how closely the reader had interpreted my aims, together with my unwritten thoughts and endeavours – I gratefully thank him for the kind compliments he has made. Such things are valued in terms better than financial gain. On November 11 by letter, I agreed to pass over my manuscript to this publisher for processing and ultimate publication. The executive editor herself undertook a 14 hour journey by train between our two locations – circumstances in which less than a couple of hours were available for discussions.

The contract specified a capital charge of £14,472. At my request this was referred back to the publisher, who agreed its reduction to £14,000 for a run of 800 books, some £3,160 less than the subsidised press publisher's price for the same manuscript at £17,160 for a 3,500 book run. Today I look back in amazement at my willingness to look at such prices,(let alone accepting them}.

On signing the contract I had omitted to take on board the corresponding size of the print runs. In this case it was 800, whereas that of Carlton Press was 3,500, which meant the capital price per book for the U.K. publisher was £17.50, whilst that of the U.S. publisher was £4.90 – roughly one-quarter the cost. I make no excuses for this lapse other than that it was careless, out of character, and an act of sheer stupidity perpetrated by someone who had developed throughout his career considerable experience in negotiating and servicing mining contracts valued at many, many thousands of pounds.

However, reflecting upon this, it does indicate the dilemma of a first-time writer lacking even the sort of background I possessed. It is quite understandable in such cases for the would-be author to rely upon the publisher to deal with the situation fairly, particularly so in view of the publisher's promotional claims already discussed. As a rough guide in such situations, I would suggest to any emerging author, in discussing his contract, that he calculates the per capital book price as the capital charge divided by the number of books to be printed (book run). Any value above £12 calls for detailed explanation. With this value, one is looking at a probable "break-even" price of £15 with which to circumvent losses arising from indirect sales and sales discounts. This highly important aspect is dealt with in much greater detail later. As costs and inflation march on, no doubt all these figures must be revised upwards in time.

However, despite having endorsed the publisher's contract with instinctive emotion rather than a cool business head, I have no reservations. It just happened, and I was jubilant. in the belief I had produced something of historical value.and put back something into the industry as a replacement for what I had received.

However, I am afraid my long production and managerial experience came to the fore time after time, in the form of of endless probing into varied situations which I felt warranted better explanation during the joint-servicing of the contract.

As I stated, I signed my publishing contract more from the heart than from the brain. There is nothing wrong in that, where the old standards of trust and honesty of intent are still retained as the coinage of staunch conduct, as experienced over many years during my long career in coal-mining. Maybe the all-too-swiftly advancing years blind one to the subtle changes which have taken place, and are taking place continuously. Such coinage apparently has no place in the modern scheme of contract negotiation and servicing when differences of legal interpretation and lack of codicil conformation" give rise to wasteful time-consuming and costly conflict, requiring a legal expert to be at one's elbow the whole time.

I make the further suggestion that one should feel free to challenge what one might consider to be capital charges substantially above a publisher's so-called average. It is understood that cases have arisen where a very high capital charge has been reduced by substantial amounts as a special concession where the author has been way out of his depth in such situations. However, in circumstances of this kind, there is always the danger of the print run being reduced both to the detriment of the author's total capital recovery, or at the expense of an uncompetitive and over-priced retail book price assessment. In view of my limited experience, one has to think that there may still be publishing houses who are still conducting business by mutual trust in terms of word, deed and bond.

What is really important about one's mistakes is that they should not be carried over into the future where one can become repetitively troubled by them. . In hindsight one often finds mistakes can turn out to have unforeseen

VANITY PRESS?
CONTRACT CONSIDERATIONS

**Publishers Capital Charges. Print Run & Retail
Book Price Determinations
At This Point Apply Simple Tests**

Per Capita Book Price = $\dfrac{\text{Capital Charge} \quad £14{,}472}{\text{Print Run Specified} \quad 800}$ = = £18.09

Breakeven Book Price = £18.09/.0.8 = £22.625/Per Copy
Query Values above £12.00 & £15.00 Per Capita &
Breakeven respectively.
Cover all agreed matters not specified in "Contract Terms"
with Jointly signed "Codicil or Affidavit".
Sleep before signing contract.
Seek professional advice on matters of grave doubt.
Good Luck in your dealings with Publisher.

merit, later adding a bonus to the joy of creative living.

If the adverse experience I have described in this exercise can be directed towards securing any member of the public against financial loss, or prevent someone making the mistakes I have outlined, I shall be well satisfied.

CONTRACTS

THE importance of the publishing contracts one signs cannot be over-stressed. I hope to demonstrate this with the help of two widely-differing examples. Ideally, contract arrangements come into being as a protective shield to both parties. However, they can be drawn up so cleverly, and be operated so ruthlessly, that the first-time writer has little practical protection after signing them, particularly if they have limited resources and are in no position to employ the best of legal brains to secure what redress their situations might call for in circumstances of contract default.

No doubt most publishers have their own version of a legally-binding agreement between themselves and an author.

Verbal gentlemen's agreements, over a handshake, unless covered by a written codicil or confirming letter to the agreement ,both duly signed and authenticated, have little chance of being honoured, if they are adverse to the publisher's interests.

Two contrasting contract documents were encountered along my route of of travel. The first defines the responsibilities of both parties in great detail, whereas the second, heavily oriented towards the publisher's interests, is much less explicit. There is a second important difference – "resolution of contract conflicts" in the American case is to be undertaken in the "civil law courts", whereas "arbitration" is the remedy reserved for the resolution of disputes in the U.K. However, this situation has been successfully challenged.

U.S.PUBLISHING CONTRACT FORMAT

WITH this format the publisher agrees to publish the author's manuscript on basis of a <u>capital charge print run and retail book price</u> all fixed and levied by the publisher. The total proceeds generated from the first edition sale of the book, less discounted sales, are shared between the author and the publisher on a 60/40 per cent basis (NB – here the publisher has a direct financial interest in the book's future, and can be expected to gear his publicity, advertising and promotional effort to that end.).

U.K- CONTRACT FORMAT

WITH this format, the publisher agrees to publish the author's manuscript on the basis of a **_capital charge and print run_** both fixed and levied upon the author by the publisher, with the **_retail book price_** later fixed by the publisher and agreed with the author. The total proceeds generated from the first edition sale of the book, 100 per cent less discounted sales, are to be vested with the author (NB: Here the publisher receives his full service charges and profits immediately the author makes his final incremental capital charge payment at the time the books are to be promoted into the public domain. Further interest in the book's public acceptance and success lies at the discretion of the publisher and his conscience. However, the book's promotion is of lesser importance to the publisher in these circumstances than would be the case with to the publicity, advertising and promotional campaign set out in the U.S. arrangements, (providing of course such are honoured).

At this stage I would ask the reader to note the pattern of the underlined values expressed in both forms of contract. They have great significance. In the first case the three values, <u>capital charge, print run and retail book price</u> are more likely to be inter-related and integrated by the publisher to provide an optimum retail book selling price. (He has 40 per cent interest in the success of the venture).

In the second case the first two are inter-related at the discretion of the Publisher. The higher he sets his capital levy and the smaller he fixes his print run charges, without proper reference to the book's competitive retail price, the more he maximises his service charge and boosts his inter-related profits at the author's expense.(and indeed indirectly, the public's expense as a result over-pricing).

This situation can have a serious and adverse effect upon the would-be author's first efforts to break into the book publishing business, in that such an approach automatically and artificially fixes the retail book price beyond an optimum value in order to achieve a break-even situation – i.e. Capital = Total Sales less discounts – in the interests of the author which he purports to have (being disappointed if he fails).

It could well be that, in many situations, as I believe with my own, that before the ink of the signatures on the contract format has dried out, wittingly or unwittingly on the basis of the higher the book's retail price, the more reluctant will be the public's attitude towards its purchase. In this way a degree of unwarranted handicap has been automatically applied, reducing the book's potential for success before the manuscript is even processed. The following four examples may illustrate that point more effectively:

Publisher fixes:- Capital Charge & Print Run

Example One:- Capital Charge - C - - £8,500. - Print Run - R = 800
Capital Cost Per Book = £8,500 / 800
= £10.625 per copy. (manoeuverable)

Example Two - Capital Charge - C - - £14,472 - Print Run - R = 800
Capital Cost Per Book = £14,472 - Print Run - 800
= £18.09 - per copy - (highly suspect)

Example Three -Actual Situation Capital Charge - C - £14,000 -

Print Run - R = 800
Capital Charge per Copy = £14,000 / 800
= £17.500 per copy (detrimental)

Example Four - Potential Current Manuscript Capital
Charge - C- £5,300 - Print Run - 2,000
Capital Charge per Copy = £5,300 / 2000
= £2.65 per copy (high potential).

This situation is examined, explained (amongst other things) and computerised in support later in this narrative.

TERMS OF U.S. CONTRACT
Omitting the preambles, let us examine the main covenants of this Agreement:

Assignment of Rights:- *The Author assigns to the Publisher the sole right to publish in book form the Author's manuscript entitled "Machinations in Coal- Mining "*

Delivery of Manuscript:- *The Author is obliged on or before the date of the "Agreement" to deliver to his Publisher a complete copy of his manuscript with all the necessary material for printing, including camera ready illustrations, if any, together with an alphabetical index if the Author wants this to be included in the book.*

Author's Copy of Manuscripts:- *The Author is obliged to have in his of her possession the original manuscript copy. The Publisher does not undertake to insure the manuscript.*

Production Schedule:- *From the effective date of this Agreement, unless the manufacture of the book is delayed by the Author, or he has failed to meet his financial commitments, the book will be produced in not more than 160 working days.*

Book Specifications:- *The Publisher shall publish the book comprising 'edited text', which is to be printed monochromatically on quality paper, with a hard-cover binding; size of volume approximately 7 x 10 inches ; book to be jacketed and printed in two colours and varnished for durability and attractiveness. a) The initial retail price shall be $ 29.95. (£18.49). The Publisher has the right without the agreement of the Author to increase the price of the book.and is under no obligation to inform the Author in doing so. b) If in the Publisher's opinion, the book requires editing to correct spelling, syntax and/or punctuation errors , The Publisher shall provide this service at no additional cost to the Author.*

Copyright and Listings:- *The Publisher shall apply for copyright of the book in the name of the Author with the Library of Congress in Washington D.C, he shall also apply for a catalogue card number for the book for the* permanent United States publishing record on file at the Library of Congress. a) So as to readily make the order information about the book available to bookstores, libraries, wholesalers, and the general public. The Publisher shall assign an International Standard Book Number (ISBN) to the book. Furthermore the Publisher shall affix a Bookland EAN and bar code to the jacket so as to make the book suitable for purchase at automated cash registers

Correction of Proofs :- The Publisher shall send the Author proofs for the book prior to printing. It is agreed that the materials in the proofs shall be the edited text of the manuscript described in Section II. The Author shall correct and return the proofs to the Publisher in a timely fashion. The Publisher shall correct any printer's errors noted by the Author on the proofs, at no charge to the Author, except as set forth below. If it is necessary to correct proofs due to alterations other than of the printer's typographical or punctuation errors, the Author shall remit the cost of such corrections in the amount of $1.00 per alteration. The Publisher shall assume no responsibility for the correction of textual errors other than those so noted by the Author even if the Author is not the party responsible for such errors;

a) The Publisher shall not print the book prior to receipt of final corrected proofs from the Author on which the Author shall have affixed his or her signature. The Author's signature on the final proof shall constitute the Author's approval that the corrected text on the final proofs is exactly the text which the Author wishes to appear in the published book.

Author's Copies:- The Publisher shall provide the Author with 100 copies of the book upon receipt of payment in full. If the Author remits payment in full upon the signing of this Agreement, the Publisher shall send the Author an additional 50 copies at no additional charge once the bound books are available. The Author may sell or give away any or all copies of the book delivered to him by the Publisher.The Author may purchase additional copies of the book at a 50 percent discount (50%) off the retail price in effect at the time of purchase.

Authors Compensation:- a) The Publisher agrees to pay the Author $19.97 (sixty per cent - 60% - of the retail price) on all paid sales made direct from the Publisher at full retail price, up to the first 3,500 copies

b) On paid sales made at a discount but not including 50% off the retail price, the Author's compensation shall be forty per cent - 40% - off the retail price

c) On paid sales at a discount of 50 per cent or more off the retail price, the Author's compensation shall be one half the rates specified in a) of this covenant specified in 9.c) and 11.

d) No compensation shall be paid to the Author for any books shipped but not paid for, sent to publications or electronic media for review, samples sent free of charge to bookstore, libraries, wholesalers or other booksellers, lost destroyed, remaindered, given away by the Author.

Fulfilment Of Orders:- The Publisher shall be responsible for the production of the book and shall fulfil all bone-fide orders received from stores, distributors merchants, organisations and the general public.

Second and Subsequent Editions:- If the Publisher's sole opinion the sale of the book warrants, the Publisher shall publish, at it's own expense, all copies printed and bound in excess of 3,500 Copies. On all paid sales of such excess copies, the Author shall receive a royalty of twenty five percent (25%) of the retail price, within specified exceptions.

Payment Of Author's Compensation:- Here the Publisher is required to provide the Author, or his representatives, a statement of sales and earned income, and to make payment of such income due to the Author no later than the last day of September and March of each year, statements and payments to the Author made at these times will reflect paid sales through to the previous six (6) month period ending June 30th and December 31st respectively

b) If at the end of any six (6) month period, the net amount due to the Author is less than fifty dollars ($50.00), the Publisher may defer the issuance of statements and payments until such time as this sum or more may be due.

c) The Author upon written request shall have the right to examine, or have the Author's duly authorized representative examine, the records of the Publisher regarding paid sales for the book which the Publisher has received..

Payments From Author To Publisher:- The Author shall agree to pay the Publisher

$9,100. with the signing of the contract
$ 9,100. with completion of editing
$ 9,100. with return of "proofs"
$ 500. Final balance;
$27,800.

Subsidiary Rights:- The Publisher shall have exclusive control of the subsidiary rights and is free to arrange for the sale thereof. If the Publisher in its sole discretion deems this to be appropriate. the proceeds of any such sale shall be divided eighty percent (80%) to the Author and 20 percent (20%) to the Publisher. These rights shall include, but not be limited to, the following; merchandising, reprint edition, publication, anthology or quotation, video presentation broadcast, television, motion picture.

In the event of any other proceeds received from any other rights such proceeds shall be divided eighty percent (80%) to the Author and twenty percent (20%) to the Publisher.

Publicity, Promotion, Advertising:- The various and several means of promoting the book, described below, are to be carried out by the Publisher without cost to the Author provided the latter has performed all of the obligations hereunder including, but not limited to, the remittance of any or all payments due the Publisher. Both Publisher and Author agree that neither party makes any representation or promise to the other with regard to future reaction from the public, the media or the market, it being impossible to predict the future reaction to or sale of a yet unpublished manuscript.

a) The Publisher shall create a news release announcing the publication of the book to be distributed along with all promotional copies of the book.

b) The Publisher shall send up to fifty (50) copies of the book, along with the copy of the news release and a solicitation to review the book, to print media, which may include newspapers, magazines, trade journals, listing sources, indexes, abstracts and other publications.

c) The Publisher shall also send promotional copies of the book and/or news releases to book sellers located in or near the Author's place of residence, along with a notice soliciting, the sale of the book, to autograph parties and window displays.

d) Details of the Publisher's co-operative advertising program shall be included with all material sent to booksellers. All interested booksellers shall be allowed to participate in the program in accordance with the Publisher's current policy.

e) The Publisher shall send promotional copies of the book and/or news releases to libraries located in or near the Author's place of residence, along with a notice soliciting the addition of the book to the library's collections, sales, autograph parties and displays.

f) The Publisher shall also send promotional copies of the book and/or news releases and a notice soliciting the sale and stocking of the book to appropriate wholesalers, distributors, jobbers or corporate headquarters of national and regional chain booksellers.

g) For the purpose of obtaining publicity, the Publisher shall send promotional copies of the book and/or news releases , and a notice soliciting interviews, personal appearances and reviews in electronic media, including radio stations and television stations in the Author's state , province or nearby area.

h) The Publisher reserves the right to send additional promotional copies of the book and/or news releases and a notice soliciting interviews and solicitation to review, purchase the book or its subsidiary rights or publicise the book to all entities of the Publisher's choice, including but not limited to specialised sales outlets, organisations, associations, awards committees, publishers and other businesses if the Publisher so deems appropriate.

i) The Publisher shall purchase an advertisement with mail-order coupon comprising up to fifty (50) agate lines in a newspaper in the Author's state or province.

j) At the Author's request, the Publisher shall produce and mail to the Author up to five hundred (500) direct mail pieces, to be sent to private individuals known to the Author. The Author may return these, duly addressed to the Publisher , who will mail them individually at no cost to the Author. Furthermore the Publisher reserves the right to issue direct mail-solicitations if the Publisher believes that the sales warrant continued efforts.

k) For the purposes of making information about the book available to bookstores, libraries, and wholesalers , the Publisher shall apply for a listing in BOOKS IN PRINT, the standard reference work used by the book selling trade. In addition the book shall be listed in the first available edition of the PUBLISHER' S TRADE LIST ANNUAL. A listing for the book shall also appear in the Publisher's catalogue.

l) The Publisher shall be responsible for the creation of all promotional material and advertising copy and content thereof. The Author's suggestions concerning any of this material shall be considered and utilised if the Publisher so deems this appropriate. However, in view of the Publisher's experience and expertise, it is agreed that all matters connected with the promotional procedures described herein shall be determined in the sole discretion of the Publisher.

m) The Publisher may grant permission to any reviewer, commentator or other entity to publish excerpts from the book for the purposes of obtaining publicity or encouraging sales.

Other Terms.

a) The Author warrants to the Publisher that he or she is the legal owner of the manuscript: that the manuscript is free from any claim of debt, public or private; that none of the manuscript violates a copyright or a common law right of others and that the manuscript contains nothing libellous or illegal. The Author will hold harmless and indemnify the Publisher in any manner of claims, proceedings and expenses (included without-limitation attorney's fees and expenses) which may arise out of breach of any representation or warranty of the Author contained herein and from any allegation that the manuscript is subject to any claim whether or not such claim might be instituted in a court of law. Upon receipt of notification of any such claim, the Publisher may withhold publication or distribution of the book.

b) In event the Author fails to perform any of the obligations herein, including but not limited to the failures to remit monies to the Publisher, the Publisher shall not be required to perform any of the activities specified herein until such time as the Author has fulfiled all required obligations and remitted any and all monies due to the Publisher.

c) In the event that the Author believes the Publisher has failed to perform any conditions specified herein, the Author shall give the Publisher notice thereof by registered mail, and if then cures any default that may actually exist within a reasonable time thereafter, the Agreement will not be deemed to have been breached.

d) The Publisher reserves the right to delete any material or text that the Publisher feels in its sole discretion would subject the book to any claim, proceeding or expense specified in Section 16 a), including but not limited to material from sources other than the Author where the Publisher deems that insufficient permission for reprint has been obtained. In all cases, the Author shall be responsible for making all necessary arrangements and payments for the inclusion in the book of material not of the Author's creation.

e) In the event that any provision of this Agreement is deemed unenforcable or invalid , no provision of this agreement shall be deemed to be affected thereby, and all other provisions shall be deemed enforceable and valid.

f) If manufacture or publication of the book is delayed by fire or water damage, material shortage, delay by any supplier or carrier charged with transmittal of proofs or other printed material to the Author or to the Publisher, or act of God, the publisher shall bear no liability for any such delay.

Terms of Agreement. The effective date of this Agreement shall be the date the Agreement is countersigned by the Publisher after the Publisher's receipt of the initial payment from the Author . The Publisher shall send to the Author after such countersignature a fully executed copy of the Agreement. The term of this Agreement shall be two and one-half years beginning with its effective date.

The Publisher may at its option extend the term of this by the Author written confirmation of such an extension not later than thirty (30) days prior to the expiration of the initial term . Upon expiration or termination of the Agreement, the Publisher shall have no further responsibility under this Agreement, except that the Author shall be sent any compensation or monies due from the Publisher the time of the next semi-annual reporting period. Furthermore the Author shall have the right to obtain any or all of the bound copies of the books in then in the Publisher's possession within thirty (30) days after the termination of this Agreement at thirty (30) percent of the current retail price, and thereafter the Publisher shall have the right to sell or otherwise dispose of any remaining books as the Publisher sees fit without obligation.

Complete Agreement. The stipulations and agreements herein shall bind the heirs, executors, administrators, successors and assignees of the Author, and successors and assignees of the Publisher. This Agreement represents the entire Agreement between the parties hereto, and the Author and the publisher agree that no representations or promises other than contained in this Agreement have been made, nor shall any such representation or promise bind either party. The Agreement shall be governed by the laws of the State of New York in all respects, including all manners of construction, validity, and performance and none of its terms or provisions may be waived or altered, except in writing signed by both parties.

Since all work performed hereunder by the Publisher shall be undertaken at its place of business in New York and its records pertaining thereto shall be maintained there, any action arising from or pertaining to this Agreement shall be instituted only in a Court in the City of New York. The Author hereby agrees to pay Publisher's cost, including all attorney's fees and expenses in obtaining dismissal of any action brought in a jurisdiction outside the City of New York in breach of this Agreement, trial by jury and consequential damages are hereby waived and it is agreed that any claim for damages by the Author shall not exceed the account paid by the Author to the Publisher prior to the time such claim is made.

I have tried to cover each provision as simply as I can but this is no substitute for the original legal instrument, nor can it be regarded as such. Its purpose is try and give the reader some idea of the sort of matters covered in or omitted from a publishing contract.

As a layman I felt its clarity was readily understandable and gave a clear idea of the schedule for publishing the book, capital costs, default time of completion, and a detailed understanding of a promotional campaign. To me it was most enlightening.

U.K. BOOK AGREEMENT

Again let us omit the preambles and consider the main features:

1. The Author has submitted the work to the Publisher complete with all illustrations and other material requisite to its publication in a book format. The Publisher agrees, subject to the terms and conditions specified in joint Agreement to publish the work with all promptitude, in any event not later than 31st October 1996, and the first edition or print run shall comprise of a total of 800 copies.

2. For the work to be done the Author agrees to make payments in a manner set out in the Schedule of Payments which form part of this Agreement and if such payments are not made, then this Agreement shall at the discretion of the Publisher become void. After the signing the Agreement should the Author decide to increase the size of the manuscript in any way or add to the number of illustrations or undertake any action or alterations with regard to the manuscript after it is already delivered to the Publisher which shall materially increase the cost of production then the Publisher may at his discretion make a substantiated surcharge to the owner. The Author shall within 28 days of such notice make payment to the Publisher of such a surcharge.

3. The ownership of the copyright in the work shall continue to be that of the Author who hereby grants the Publisher a licence to publish one edition of the work. All other rights shall remain the property of the respective owner.

4. The Author warrants to the Publisher that the work contains nothing of libellous, obscene or blasphemous nature and that it is in no way an infringement of the copyright of any other party and that any permission he may have obtained shall be available for inspection by the Publisher. In the event of the Publisher suffering loss as a result of any default on the part of the Author then the Author shall indemnify the Publisher for all such loss or damage.

5. The Publisher shall:

(i) edit, proof read, design the cover and set and bind the work at such typesetters, printers and binders he shall consider to be the most economic and able to give the best service as he shall at his discretion decide.

(ii) be responsible for the general promotion and sales campaign and/or the work involved. He shall use to his best endeavours in consultation with the Author to sell as many copies as possible and shall with the agreement of

the Author fix the retail price of the book. He shall also send out review copies in consultation with the Author as shall be appropriate. He shall invoice and dispatch all copies sold to the trade and to individual purchases of copies and shall account to the Author such commissions as appropriate within three months of their receipt other than in the case of books which are sold on a sale-or-return basis.

(iii) ask the Author to read either galley proof and /or page proofs of the book and on the galley proofs make such correction as necessary, but on the page proofs shall confine such corrections to spelling and punctuation only. Should the Author find it necessary at the galley or page proof stage to alter the work in such a way as to increase the publisher's costs in excess of £10 then the Publisher at his discretion shall request the Author to pay such excess.

(iv) in the event of re-printing the work being mutually agreed, draw up a new agreement, and pay all expenses of such a re-print from which the Author shall receive a royalty of not less than 15 percent.

(v) carry the cost of all warehousing and the invoicing and dispatch of all books purchased from the Publisher and at all times maintain accurate stock records which shall be available to the Author.

(vi) dispatch the necessary copies to the copyright libraries and be entitled to four copies of the work for his own purpose.

(vii) in the event of his failure to publish the book with all due promptitude and in the event not later than 31st October 1996 unless for reasons beyond his control or with the agreement of the Author, and on request of the Author, return to the Author all monies paid to him by the Author as set out in the Schedule hereto.

6. (a) If the Publisher fails to fulfil or comply with any of the provisions of the contract within one month after notification from the Author of such failure, or if the Publisher goes bankrupt or into liquidation or has a Receiver appointed, the contract shall automatically terminate and the rights granted shall revert to the Author.

(b) When the work goes out of print or off the market the contract shall terminate and all rights granted shall revert to the Author. Terminations under (a) or (b) shall be without prejudice to:

(i) any claims which the Author may have for monies due at the time of termination and

(ii) any claims the Author may have against the Publisher in respect of breaches by Publisher in the terms of this Agreement.

7. In the event of disagreement between any of the parties hereto, arbitrators shall be appointed in accordance with the laws of England.

Having presented both types of contract – maybe one can develop personal views thereon – It will be noted that the U.K. contract, although more simple to follow, is much less specific than the forgoing U.S. contract. It could well be (and I believe it to be so) that the larger of the U.K publishing houses, not like the American publishers, have drawn up and operate on much more detailed covenanted contracts than the one above.

However, I believe this form of U.K. contract to be substantially oriented towards the publishers in such a way as to place them in a highly secure situation – one in which in spite of the validity of an author's grievance, he has but little chance of redress, particular with any publisher's failures to effectively and adequately promote his work.

Clause 5 (ii) requires him to be responsible for the "promotion and sales campaign" and to use his best endeavours in consultation with the author to sell as many copies as possible.

The importance to an author of the promotional aspects of a contract cannot be over-stressed. The comparative fundamental differences between the two contracts are summarised below, from which it can be observed that the U.K. contract format addresses little enforceable magnitude to the aspect of a book's promotion.

FUNDAMENTAL CONTRACT COMPARISONS
UNITED STATES OF AMERICA UNITED KINGDOM CONTRACT

	USA	UK
Author responsible for cost of publication	✔	✔
Cost of publication	£17,160	£14,000
	($27,800)	($22,680)
Quotation for A4 size	n/a	£16,995
		($27,532)
Print run (copies)	3,500	800
Retail selling price	£18.48	£23.25
	($29.95)	$37.67)
		(final agreed price)
Capital cost per copy	£4.90	£17.50
	($7.94)	($28.35)
Book specification	Hardcover	Paperback
	179mm x 276mm	156mm x 254mm
Production schedule	160 working days	29/11/95 31/10/96
		(335 calendar days)
		Actual release
		31/12/96
		(381 calendar days)
Other condition	Clearly defined terms	Restated to publication responsibilities to general promotion and sales campaign
Period of agreement	2.5 years	None specified

My comment on the American contract is that it is far more informative and precise in what is to be undertaken, more particularly so in terms of promotional activity. With the U.S. publisher I first picked, one has to accept his contract (and his integrity and commitment) on trust, but there is a greater measure of detail in the contract in support thereof. The Publisher has almost an equally joint engagement, and what should flow from that is a much stronger desire to maximise a book's success.

However, despite all I have outlined above, the American experience with the subsidised press publisher is apparently no different from that of the United Kingdom involvement with a vanity press publisher.

Here are some of the difficulties which beset the U.K. author trying to have a book published through a subsidised press publisher in the United States:

A subsidy press will often rave over an author's work, and offer to contribute 50 per cent of the production and marketing costs – but only if the writer will cover the remainder. Usually the amount he is expected to meet is actually more than it would have been to have the book packaged correctly.

The author who has paid for an entire run actually receives only a fraction of the alleged "press run" and must purchase additional copies from the publisher

Sometimes the author is promised a royalty based on a percentage after a certain number of copies are sold.

The subsidy press offers to list books in its catalogue or to send out some press releases or flyers. Little, if any, success obtains from the former, whilst the latter is something well within the province of the author's capabilities.

They are forthright about the fact that the author is responsible for subsidising the project, and in return will receive 40 per cent of the retail price as compensation, if any copies are sold. Brochures examined indicate that a little-known author is hard to sell and that marketing efforts are limited to press releases and catalogues – the information being sandwiched between glowing testimonials which imply that subsidy presses successfully sell books.

There are many variations on these themes, but in essence the bottom line is that the author pays a lot and doesn't get much in return.

PROCESSING

A contract drawn up on the U.K. format was agreed upon and signed by the author and the executive editor on behalf of the publisher, this procedure being duly observed and.certified by an attendant witness on November 29, 1995. Thus the project was set in motion. Three days later confirmation of the book's specification was received.

Royal Octavo Size – 234mm by 158mm
Text and Photographs –Standard Arrow 80 GSM Paper
Two Tone Outer Cover – 93 Black and White Illustrations

Acknowledgments covered the initial payment, revised manuscript and a full.set of drawings, and photographs.

PROCESSING STAFF
BASICALLY the following heads of staff convert the manuscript into its final book form, prior to its submission to the final operation of printing and binding – editor, typesetter, publishing manager, artist, promotions manager, promotions co-ordinator.

Their inter-related duties need to be organised to the best effect such that a book's production flow within the general current of the total manuscript stream can be undertaken with the minimum disruption to the whole situation and the least amount of delay or disturbance.

As with most systems involving the efficient production of a commodity or the smooth running of a service, experience has dictated the need for well thought out and highly developed production schedules. In my former career as a mining engineer the range over which such schedules extended was indeed wide and all-embracing. It was no surprise for me to receive one such production schedule in relation to the activities and periods covering the different aspects of the book's production.

A copy is shown overleaf:

TITLE OF BOOK : Machinations in Coal-mining
AUTHOR : Charles Round
ISBN: 1 85821 403 3

Manuscript to Editor:- 14.12.1995
Copy Edited manuscript to Typesetter 22.01.1996
Author's Questionnaire 23.01.1996
Galley proofs to Publisher from Typesetter 04.03.1996
Galley proofs to Author and Editor 05.03.1996
Author's corrected galleys to Publisher..25.03.1996
Author's corrected galleys to Editor 26.03.1996
Promotion package preparation commences................................07.04.1996
Artist briefed on Jacket Design 07.04.1996
Master galleys to Publisher from Editor 08.04.1996
Master galleys to Typesetter 09.04.1996
Jacket Visuals for Author to approve 04.05.1996
Page proofs to Publisher from Typesetter 06.05.1996
Page proofs to Author and Editor 07.05.1996
Author's jacket recommendations to Publisher 07.05.1996
Author's jacket recommendations to Artist 08.05.1996
Author corrected page proofs to Publisher 27.05.1996
Author corrected page proofs to Editor 28.05.1996
Master page proof to Publisher from Editor 10.06.1996
Master page proof to Typesetter..11.06.1996
Finished jacket artwork to publisher from Artist..........................28.06.1996
Camera-ready copy and artwork to Printer 01.07.1996
Advance copies delivered ....05.08 .1996
Promotion Package initiated 19.08.1996
Publication Date. 21.10.1996

Whilst every effort is made to adhere to these dates, delays do sometimes

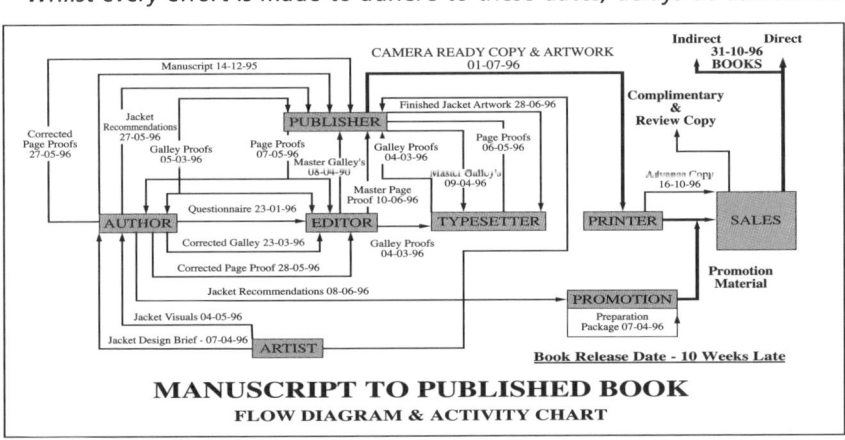

MANUSCRIPT TO PUBLISHED BOOK
FLOW DIAGRAM & ACTIVITY CHART

occur and.this can therefore only be treated as an approximate timescale.

Throughout a long career in both lower and higher management situations in the National Coal Board I was often placed in the situation of being held to account and holding staff to account on matters of schedules related to actual production.

To me a production schedule assumes the importance of a control document in that it identifies delay and failure. Used effectively it exposes things that have gone wrong, or are likely to go wrong, particularly useful in situations where this led to senior management follow-ups and calls for explanations followed by effective action. This is necessary to sort out and eliminate problems which adversely affect the production flow cycle, particularly where failure to take corrective action arises and the same problem or problems constantly recur.

The last sentence, at the end of the publisher's production schedule above ,attempts to introduce some flexibility and tolerance into the situation. Being a negative approach, it becomes a statement which reduces such an important administrative instrument's effectiveness.

However, it can have some effect in keeping off potential author enquiries. Where failures occur by reason of external matters "directly beyond the control of the.responsible authority or authorities", experience indicates clear and detailed.explanations are readily on hand. With failures arising from "management and organisational lapses" that is an entirely different matter, in which case such reference has strong connotations of an excuse, or the acceptance of a low efficiency operation.

In the event, the first production schedule failed to be achieved. This was followed by a second revised production schedule carrying the same pre-excuse. That too failed to such a degree that the contract default deadline of October 31 1996 also failed to be met. This required of me a dispensation accepting the situation so that the work could continue.

It would seem no matter how many times failures to meet production deadlines occurred, the same disclaimer would be applied, reducing the position to one of travesty.

Under the contract conditions, ostensibly I was at that point in a position to demand the return of all monies paid to the publisher. Viewing the situation in practical.manner I believe the contract to be so heavily oriented in the publisher's favour that the chances of achieving this are highly remote. Moreover, intensifying the risks could well involve additional heavy expenditure with little chance of success, irrespective of the merits involved.

On the basis of the production schedule above, the rough flow diagram was designed for the purpose of developing an overall chart-form view of the manuscript's movements during processing to the point of public projection in the final book form. With access to greater detail than is expressed in the schedule above, in the absence of factual acceptable explanation of the inability to meet forecasts and deadlines, there is a vital need to have the whole situation investigated in great depth.

Subjecting schedules of the above nature into a "diagrammatic flow situation" often opens up avenues of approach whereby bottlenecks are eliminated, enabling a process.to be streamlined towards cost reduction and greater overall efficiency. The inter-relationship of the author within the scheme of things is clearly shown:

In the very early stages it was discovered the time scale had but little chance of being achieved – a situation which led me to enquire if any problems were being encountered. However the response dealt only in generalities and mentioned nothing specific, indicating to me the publisher attached little importance to the delays.

Throughout the whole project there were signs, time after time, which caused me to feel the publisher's organisation was not so dynamic as I would have expected it to be. Generalities may serve to pacify those not so well experienced in management, no matter what commercial or industrial discipline, but to those having served a long apprenticeship therein over many, many years, such generalities are accepted as little more than excuses, and have little to contribute to the build-up of a highly efficient and profitable enterprise.

If I am correct in my assumptions, it could explain why in one agreement six months in the publication of a manuscript is the satisfactory norm, in another similar situation a publisher projects approximately eight months for the work. Undertaking the project through a packager can be even quicker.

Such thoughts and views expressed expose the presumptuous author to the heavy criticism of showing a lamentable lack of knowledge with regard to the book publishing industry. Obviously those who are so knowledgeable are less likely to be taken for a ride.

Since the days of the William Caxton printing press of 1477– as with other commercial and.manufacturing disciplines – revolutionary advances have been made, particularly in the last 40 years, with the advance of the computer and development of suitable software. Surely the time is approaching whereby the projection of a manuscript, its processing and completion is undertaken in but a fraction of the time now taken, if it is not with us already? This line of thought, incidentally, caused me to wonder how many authors are fully informed of all events, to their satisfaction, after submitting their manuscripts. Maybe I am not alone in such matters.

In the very early days of my career I drew up a substantial number of colliery notices and posted instructions, among a wide range of other duties, using a small printing press. With the lead characters that then had to be used, combined with the black printer's ink of the times, it was one hell of a messy, unpleasant and slow job!

I firmly believe that to accept things as they are, rather than to seek to introduce beneficial changes by bringing into play the vital elements of intellect and imagination within a corporate body, is a sure way of falling behind in the current highly competitive world – a world in which such change is being introduced in many commercial and industrial situations at a somewhat exponential rate.

Recently I had the privilege of examining some excellent high quality books, marketed at highly competitive prices, produced in China. After all the Far East has taken over the Western dominance in the manufacture of radios, televisions, hi-fi equipment, cars and other products. The capacity is apparently there which can and will be developed in the publishing business.

However it could well be that our leading commercial publishing houses are among the best-equipped and most efficient anywhere, and that these mainstream houses accept change and development in all its aspects.

In this respect I recall my first managerial appointment at Rotherham Main Colliery in South Yorkshire. In January 1947, some 300 men produced 1,500 tons per 45-hour 6-day week In August 1996, at the Cyprus Amax Mineral Company's Twentymile Mine, Englewood, Colorado, US, the same number of men were producing at the rate of 4,000-5,000 tons per hour, effecting the production of 1,000,000 tons from one mechanised installation in the month of August 1997, based upon a mining system I had formerly pioneered and developed in 1969/70. Food for thought!

PROCESSING DIFFICULTIES ENCOUNTERED
The first problem encountered was raised by the typesetter on March 11th, 1996. He had discovered some discrepancy between the on-screen documents and the printed text and had trouble deciphering the captions to be used with the illustrations (floppy disks containing all the text and graphics were given to the publishes along with the original manuscript).

This I could understand, although to me it wasn't particularly worrying. An offer to travel to Preston, Lancashire, to resolve the problem in the early stages was not accepted. Eventually, in the course of proof reading, I was able to effect resolution in a matter of a few hours. Since a number of sequence photographs projected a particular mining system or approach, it was necessary to treat the associated captions in a manner which departed somewhat from the normal arrangement of individual captions matching individual pictures. My own time allocations in terms of length, although affected by the publisher's delays, were met with regard to the proofs, master proofs, and a final set of revised proofs as they were made available to me.

Progress, however, fell behind in all aspects of the former production schedule. This I found difficult to understand in that although there is an apparent high degree of sequential activity, other parts of the work not affected by any particular problem could be prepared normally as projected and later injected at the correct point of time. Promotional packages involving a fair degree of duplication between manuscripts are a case in point. I am afraid my former production, managerial and administrative training caused me to be far more critical and frustrated than would generally have been the case with other authors having lesser experience within those fields.

In my former situation I was able to follow-up staff failures directly as they came to notice and initiate corrective action almost immediately. In this new situation and under its prevailing circumstances, any attempt that could or might be made to influence the outcome had strict limitations.

Completion dates for any activity I was involved in have always, to me, been sacrosanct. Production schedules loosely constructed, and apparently acceptably so, in the course of time become less meaningful and eventually of little real value in securing efficient administration.

Observing that progress in relation to the original production schedule activities was heading for serious shortfalls of achievement I put in a protest which gave rise to a revised publication date of October 21 1996, (ten days short of the contract's default date, October 31) which in the event was not achieved.

A meeting was sought with the publisher at his offices in mid-July 1996 motivated by the circumstances above.

The first round trip travelling about 700 miles between my home and the publisher's headquarters was undertaken with help and support of my nephew's wife, Mrs Dorothy Round, a former deputy school headmistress.

We met the executive editor and the publishing manager over some two hours, coming to terms with the fact the publication date would be delayed. This situation gave rise to a great deal of consternation and emotional feeling. It was somewhat like trying to catch a ghostly shadow. While attempting to seek clarity and find out what the problems really were, generalities, evasions and no mention of anything specific seemed to be the stock approach.

The experiences I encountered influenced me to believe things are so secure and unchangeable in favour of the publisher operating the type of contract that I had entered into, that the author doesn't have a great deal of protection.

MARKETING CONSIDERATIONS

Number of Books–First Edition–The size of the market for any particular book in question (considering all aspects of the books likely appeal etc), and the volume of the *'first edition'* stock in terms of retail book sales likely to be disposed of within that market, determines a basic risk factor.

The greater the allocated *"print run"* (number of books chosen for the *"first edition"* the higher the risk of unsold copy and lost revenue associated therewith. With the pitching of the number of books likely to form that *"first edition stock"* too low one faces a situation of increased production cost and higher *"book retail prices"* which as previously stated adversely affects the books competitive prospects, relative to both *"break-even and/or profit margins"*..

Production Cost–The problem here is to determine the cost level at which the chosen volume of *"first edition book stock level"* can be produced. Here two basic factors are involved:

MANUSCRIPT "FIRST EDITION" CONTRACTS ELEMENTAL VALUES

Book Title –   "Machinations in Coal Mining"
            IBSN – 1-85821-403-3

Element Cost Per Copy	Book Specifications
Editorial £1237 £1.56	Paperback:-Royal Octavo 234 x 158mm
Typesetting £4062 £5.08	Text & Photo's –Standard Arrow 80 GSM
Jacket Design & £1234 £1.54 Production	Two Tone Cover Black & White Illustrations Illustrations
Printing & Binding £4646 £5.82	Photo's Figures Plans Charts 68 15 5 7
Administration £1730 £2.36	Pages – 399 Copies 800
Promotion £1563 £1.93	Per Capita Copy Price £18.09
TOTALS £14,472 £18.O9	Breakeven Book Price £22.6215
	Pitched Retail Book Price £23.25

Author's Potential Profit - 800 Books @ (£23.25 – £22.62) = £510.00

ACTUAL SITUATION

The Opening Book Stock was 732 Copies - an unexplained shortfall of 68 copies
Voluntary, Promotional Copy & Statutory Copy – attracts no revenue – 32 such
copies involved

Effective Revenue Print Run   = (732-32) x 0.80 = 560
Maximum Revenue Generation =   560 x £23.25 = £13,020

Potential Losses on Publishers Projected Contract Proposals
                = (£14472-£13020 = £1,452 loss)
On the basis all 732 copies disposed of in the manner indicated – 50%
sales split &40% discount on indirect retail avenue sales & all copy sold

(i) **Non Repetitive Cost:-** the total cost of converting the manuscript into its finalised form, ready for 'printing and binding'–this includes all processing salaries, materials, initial promotional expenditure as contained within the publisher's following: breakdown:

The above represents the publisher's original *"cost build-up"* version in relation to the accepted "total contract price" when the contract was signed – at the time of which the publisher's agent by phone obtained permission to reduce the amount by £472 to £14,000.

The publisher's profits are not shown, being contained but hidden within the above detailed analysis, otherwise he operates on a *"non-profit or loss"* making basis. This particular build-up calls for a great deal of analysis if it is to be accepted and taken as a serious portrayal of the true and fair situation.

(ii) **Repetitive cost-Second and subsequent Editions:-** Here we are concerned with those costs which are actually involved in re-printing the **'first edition'** (assuming this to be a self-contained project with which to test the market). It represents the basic costs associated with printing and binding, in the production of a fixed number of books, together with miscellaneous costs, such as those involved in further promotion, publicity etc.

(iii) **Profit or loss:-** In simple terms, profit obtains where the Total Book Sales (revenue) exceed the Total Costs of Production (costs). Losses occur where the total costs of production exceed the total book sales (revenue).

Elementary could well be your correct reaction – quite so. However, matters are not quite so simple – particularly from the aspect of accurate forecasting and the determination of potential sales or profit. The basic difficulty lies with the public's degree of interest in, and demand for, the title, following release into its domain.

To influence that interest with the object of *"maximising"* demand, many things can be undertaken with varying degrees of success or failure. First and foremost is the book's natural appeal to potential readers, secondly its presentation, quality and price, and thirdly, the stimulation of that interest by effective promotional activity. The latter embraces the media, retail and mail order outlets. Such a situation gives rise to range of variable factors both in terms of *"direct distribution (mail order) and indirect distribution (retail outlets)"* involving compensation, usually individually agreed as a percentage discount on a book's retail price. With the *"national retail outlets"* this can be more than 40 per cent of the books price. At this point I believe there is a serious anomaly both from the author's, publishers and public point of view. The current arrangement of **"discounts on the total retail price of a book"** needs to be replaced by an arrangement which is much more fair to all concerned. Please bear with me, I believe it to be highly important. This element is basically a cost of servicing the book's promotion and distribution, and should be regarded as such with a standard code of treatment developed. Let us examine the situation in the light of my personal experience. Two examples of potential profitability are developed:-

1. Example One–This represents the "publishers assessments–"ad hoc" in the sense the three basic contract elements–*"capital charge, print run, and book retail price,"* appear to have been produced by guesswork, having no true financial and mathematical relationships and which formerly projected *"heavy potential financial loss to the author,"* I have no doubt what-so-ever this situation was *"over capitalised"*, whatever the reason, maximising of profits, ineptitude, or just in-efficient management, or downright carelessness. I don't know!!, but what is obvious to me is that there is a *"knock on effect"*, penalising to the author, but at the same time gratuitous to the book retailer.

The fact that a retailers discounts are tied to a *"book's retail price"* means they are also *"directly proportional"* to the author's *"costs of production or capital changes"* which are included therein. In the case of unknown and emergent "first edition" writers they should ensure before a contract is signed by the simple test below that what is being offered is equitable and fair:-

$$\frac{\text{Capital Charge}}{\text{Print Run}} = \begin{array}{l}\textbf{A Per Capita Book Price which stands}\\ \textbf{a chance of holding its position in a highly}\\ \textbf{competitive market place}\end{array}$$

If you would like to refine this in terms of a "Breakeven retail book price" a rough guide is expressed as:-

$$\frac{\text{Per Capital Book Price}}{0.80} = \begin{array}{l}\textbf{Breakeven Price - which takes into account}\\ \textbf{a 50 percent sales split and a 40 percent}\\ \textbf{discount on indirect sales}\end{array}$$

2. Example Two–This is representative of my personal approach in the light of experience gained. Points arising include:

1. The Capital Charge is £5,000 which is 36 per cent of the former value
2. The "per capita and Breakeven" values are respectively £3.33 and £17.70, -£4.16 & £21.875. The fixed retail book prices are £7.99 and £23.25
3. The Print Run is 1,500 copies–compared with the former 800 copies
4. Retailer and Authors Profits per capita copy–£2.29 and £1.53 compared with £9.00 and £1.85
5. Capital Charge are recovered with the sale of 650 copies, leaving 850 copies as a highly flexible promotional and profit potential
6. As a "first edition" writer promotional support from **the "big retail outlets"** was minimal–no books were displayed on their stands or book shelves, or encouragement given–regardless of being a work of important historic quality (authoritive expressed opinion–not my personal one.) They merely processed orders we directed to them, on a minimum risk taking basis.

In view of its great importance this aspect is dealt with more fully in the addendum, which treats the situation in very great depth working from simple first principles to the more sophisticated manipulations of the variables associated with the publishing of books.

The author, buoyed with exuberance after his manuscript has been accepted, looks at the demand for his creation through a different pair of spectacles than does the publisher. One thing is for sure – unless public interest is stimulated, no book stands any chance of reaching the degree of success it might well achieve. That public interest has to be created in one form or another.

I would expect the publisher to prudently look, on the author's behalf, to secure the lowest level of loss that can to be carried in the worst scenario – however, certainly not at the expense of an **"optimum capital - print run retail book price relationship"**, particularly as there are now wider avenues for the disposal of excess and remaindered copies at acceptable discounted prices.

There really is a problem here in fixing at acceptable *"first edition"* levels. As discussed earlier, the financial ramifications are quite extensive. What can the publisher do to influence such a situation? It seem obvious he or she should seek to *'project all efforts towards creating the widest possible public interest'*. Not so easy where *'promotional investment'* is strictly limited (for whatever reason).

Even with heavy promotional investment, be it in books, films, plays, newly designed manufactured products or services, failures do come about regardless. Effective advertising, whatever form it takes – radio, TV, chat shows – has had quite a measure of success.

However, thinking more in global terms rather than confined national ones, i.e. exploring the possibilities of *"WWW Internet"* might be a useful approach–I believe that, as the future unfolds, the power of this media will expand at unpredictable rates. I have already developed a "temporary w.w.web site" currently under refinement. Although the publisher claims to have projected the book through the Amazon Corporation on the "WWW Internet" it falls far short of what it could have been with joint consultation. Moreover there has been no response in terms of purchases that I am aware of.

Before starting my journey of discovery within the fields of book publishing, I had developed substantial experience in certain mining locations in Europe and the United States of America and with this wider area of influence open to consideration–my manuscript was developed in-lay person terms to meet that situation, hence the number of illustrations and more detailed captions within the manuscript being used to achieve the maximum of public interest..

COMPUTER AIDS TO BOOK PRICE FORECASTS

The importance of the basic elemental factors within a publishing contract have already been discussed. Here I would like to show in what manner such concern expressed could be manifest to the first-time writer attempting to gain recognition for his or her efforts, and the recovery of the capital he expends in that direction. There are a number of mathematically-related factors, manipulation of which provides for assessments to be determined, upon which decisions can be taken.

Probably the most basic of these is the capital charge the would be author needs to generate to convert a manuscript into book format and project the finished product for sale in the market place.

Whilst the author would like to profit from this investment, he or she is anxious to recover this investment irrespective of gain and avoid loss. The factors involved in this situation have the following relationship:

Capital charge £s = First edition total costs (inclusive of publisher's profits).

Capital Charge   = Total Print Run X Adjusted Retail Book Value*

*after the financial value of the complimentary, promotional copy, sales split, and indirect sales discounts, etc are taken into consideration and the necessary adjustments made.

Promotional copy, and percentage discount rates allowed, generally are at the discretion of the publisher.

The values generally allocated to these factors are ostensibly fixed by the publisher, irrespective of mathematical relationships. In this situation, if two of the values (variables) are known the third can be calculated. Hence forecasting can be applied to determine the likelihood of achievement within a range of allocated variables.

Viewed in that light, I believe the above has a great deal to offer in this particular field of vanity publishing, both in terms of projection and the control of publisher's exploitation and excesses – gravely detrimental to an author's interests.

CAPITAL CHARGE - PRINT RUN & RETAIL BOOK PRICE COMPUTATIONS
SPREADSHEET "BASIC-£'S" PROGRAM NUMBER - 1

COMPUTER PRINTOUT No.1	Values Variables	Direct Sales	Indirect Sales	Total Sales	Total Product Costs	Profit Loss 1st	2nd Edit Profit Loss
U.K. FORMAT IN £'S STERLING							
VARIABLES		£'S	£'S	£'S	£'S	£	£
AUTHOR'S CAPITAL CHARGE £'S	14,000	7,200.00	4,320.00	11,520.00	4,000.00	-2,480.00	7,520.00
PRINT RUN - NUMBER OF BOOKS	800						
Books Capital Cost Price - £'s:-	17.50						
DISCOUNT PERCENTAGE - %:-	40.00						
DIRECT SALES PERCENTAGE. %	50.00						
Indirect Sales Percentage.-	50.00						
Direct Sales - Number of Books:-	400						
Indirect Sales - Number of Books:-	400						
PRODUCTION COST/BOOK £'S:-	£5.00						
BOOKS RETAIL COST PRICE - £'S	18.00						
UK / USA RATES £1 = $x	1.62						
AUTHORS PROFIT PERCENTAGE	100.00	7,200.00	4,320.00	11,520.00	14,000.00	-2,480.00	£1,128.00
Publishers Profit Percentage:-	0.00	0.00	£0.00	£0.00	£0.00	£0.00	£6,392.00

Note:-

This is the straight-forward "contract sitation" in which the First Time Author assumes the potential sale of 800 books. Here the "Publishers" values of £14,000 Capital - 800 print run and a requested confirmation of the books retail price at £18.00 have been taken. There is potential loss of £2,480 at the time the contract was signed before a book had been printed. Now turn over and see what the actual situation would have been in the actual circumstances which prevailed.

COMPUTER SPREADSHEET PROGRAMME NO.1 – PRINTOUT NUMBER ONE

Originally developed for the purpose of forecasting Sales & Profit Performance Levels relating to the U.K. Publisher's Specified and Other Values of Capital, Print Run, & Retail Book Price Values

CAPITAL CHARGE - PRINT RUN & RETAIL PRICE COMPUTATIONS
SPREADSHEET "BASIC-£'S" PROGRAM NUMBER - 1

COMPUTER PRINTOUT No.1	Values Variables	Direct Sales	Indirect Sales	Total Sales	Total Product Costs	Profit Loss 1st	2nd Edit Profit Loss
U.K. FORMAT IN £'S STERLING							
		£'S	£'S	£'S	£'S	£	£
VARIABLES							
AUTHOR'S CAPITAL CHARGE £'S	14,000	6,3540.00	3,812..40	10,166.40	3,530.00	-3,833.60	6,636.40
PRINT RUN - NUMBER OF BOOKS	706						
Books Capital Cost Price - £'s:-	19.83						
DISCOUNT PERCENTAGE - %:-	40.00						
DIRECT SALES PERCENTAGE. %	50.00						
Indirect Sales Percentage:-	50.00						
Direct Sales - Number of Books:-	353						
Indirect Sales - Number of Books:-	353						
PRODUCTION COST/BOOK £'S:-	£5.00						
BOOKS RETAIL COST PRICE - £'S	18.00						
UK / USA RATES £1 = $x	1.62						
AUTHORS PROFIT PERCENTAGE	100.00	6,354.00	3,812.40	10,166.40	14,000.00	-£3,833.60	£995.46
Publishers Profit Percentage:-	0.00	0.00	£0.00	£0.00		£0.00	£5,640.94

Note:-

The "capital charge & print run" taken had been fixed by the publisher who later requested me to confirm his "retail book price" of £18.00. Here is what would have been the position with all 800 books sold. A loss of £2,480. "Actually there wasn't 800 copies to sell!" Statutory copyright, complimentary, file, promotional copy amounted to 32, thus increasing the potential loss. In accordance with the Publishers "balance of books" statement, the basic opening stock was 738. Taking all these matters into consideration the Potential Loss becomes £3,383. One may ask "how could such a situation have developed within a well managed organisation."

COMPUTER SPREADSHEET PROGRAMME NO.1 – PRINTOUT NUMBER TWO

Originally developed for the purpose of forecasting Sales & Profit Performance Levels relating to the U.K. Publisher's Specified and Other Values of Capital, Print Run, & Retail Book Price Values
Print Run Reduced from 800 to 706 which with statutory copy, and an unexplained shortfall of 62 copies a more representative situational set of true values is provided

67

Under the contract terms of the U.K. format, the publisher has responsibility for fixing the retail book price which he then has to agree with the author. On being asked by the publishing manager on August 13, 1996, to confirm a retail price of £18, (the basis of which was not disclosed) on the grounds of a fixed capital charge - £14,000 – and a print run of 800, the under-noted profitability calculations as set out in simple stages, were carried out.

These determinations take into account the various rates of discounts, involved with the sale of book copies through the publishing industry's retail sales outlets. The direct mail-order sales are generally treated at about 50 per cent of the total print run, whereas the rate of discount on the booksellers' retail sales maybe anything up to 45 percent (maybe more in some cases),of the book's fixed retail price.

The calculations which follow represent my actual situation, and are based upon:

1. Author's Capital Charge = £14,000.00 = **C Capital Charge**
   Publisher's Retail Price = £18.00 = **Rp Retail Price**
   First Edition Book Limit = 800 copies = **N Print Run**
   Direct Sales Percentage = 50% = **Ds (Indirect Sales=100-Ds)**
   Indirect Sales Percentage = 50% = **Is Indirect Sales 5**
   Sales Discount % = 40% = **Sd Sales Discount %**

Contract Provisions:

Case 1:- Direct Sales = 100% assuming all 800 books sold, no complimentary and /or promotional copies given, retail book discounts not applicable.

$$\text{Book Price Per Capita} = \frac{C}{N} = \frac{\text{Capital Charge}}{\text{Print Run}} = \frac{£14000}{800} = £17.50$$

Total Revenue = **Retail Price x Number of Books**
(Publisher's retail price assessment.= £18.00)
Rp x N = £18.00 *800 = £14,400

Apparent Profit:- =Total Revenue - Capital Charge:-
=£14,400 - £14,000 = £400.

On the basis of 100 percent direct sales the retail book price of £18 looks quite safe, but this is an illusion in that wider sales outlets are required. Book stores, booksellers, distributors and other sources of book disposal, need to be used. Payment for their services takes the form of discounting the retail book price.

Actual Situation: Opening Stock   738

BASIC PROJECTION – SALES & PROFITABILITY IN $ DOLLARS
Profits – $

VARIABLES U.K. FORMAT IN £'S STERLING	Values	Direct Sales	Indirect Sales	Total Sales	Production Costs	+/- Capital Recovery 27800.00	Profit or Loss 2nd Edition
			$'S	$'S	$'S	$'S	$'S
a) AUTHOR'S CAPITAL CHARGE $'S b) PRINT RUN - NUMBER OF BOOKS	27800 3500	52,413	31,448	83,860 £51,765	27,800 £17,160	56,060 £34,605	66,535 £41,071
c) BOOKS RETAIL PRICE $'S d) DISCOUNT SALES PERCENTAGE e) DIRECT SALES PERCENTAGE % f) PRODUCTION COSTS $'S	29.95 40.00 50.00 4.95		USA Contract "Relating To Machinations in Coal Mining"				
g) CAPITAL COST PER BOOK $'S INDIRECT SALES PERCENTAGE:-	7.94 50.00						
Direct Sales – Number of Books:- Indirect Sales – Number of Books:-	1750	Turn over to see the effects of selling a maximum of 800 copies					
PROFIT DISTRIBUTION AUTHOR'S % PUBLISHER %	60 40	31,448 20,965	18,869 12,579	50,316 33,544			39,921 26,614

COMPUTER SPREADSHEET PROGRAMME NO.1 – PRINTOUT NUMBER THREE
Originally developed for the purpose of forecasting Sales & Profit Performance Levels relating to the U.S.A.
Publisher's Specified and Other Values of Capital, Print Run & Retail Book Price Values
The situation relating to the American Contract Version for the identical manuscript in which the Capital is $27000.
Print Run 3500 and Retail Book Price if $29.95

BASIC PROJECTION $'s – SALES & PROFITABILITY ON THE SALE OF BOOKS
BOOKS SOLD = 800

VARIABLES / U.S. FORMAT IN $ DOLLARS	Values	Direct Sales $'S	Indirect Sales $'S	Total Sales $'S	Production Costs $'S	Profit or Loss $'S
AUTHOR'S CAPITAL CHARGE $'S	27820	11,998.00	7,192.80	19,180.80	27,820	-8,639.20
PRINT RUN - NUMBER OF BOOKS	3500	£7,400	£4,440	£11,840	£17,173	-£5,333
BOOKS RETAIL PRICE $'S	£7.95					
DISCOUNT SALES PERCENTAGE %	40					
DIRECT SALES PERCENTAGE %	50	USA Contract "Relating To Machinations in Coal Mining"				
f) PRODUCTION COSTS $'S	4.95					
BOOKS SOLD	800	Profitability on The Sale of 800 Copies				
INDIRECT SALES PERCENTAGE:-	50					
Direct Sales – Number of Books:-	400					
Indirect Sales – Number of Books:-	400					
BOOKS RETAIL COST PRICE $'S	29.97					
PRODUCTION COST PER BOOK $'S	7.95					
UK-USA EXCHANTE RATE £=	1.62					
AUTHOR'S PROFIT PERCENTAGE	60.00	£4,440	£2,664	£7,104	£10,304	-£3,200
PUBLISHER PROFIT PERCENTAGE	40.00	£2,960	£1,766	£4,736	£6,869	-£2,133

COMPUTER SPREADSHEET PROGRAMME NO.1 – PRINTOUT NO.3
Profitability & Sales According to Books Sold

PUBLISHERS BOOK BALANCE SHEET

Copies to Author 634	File Copy 1
Total Accounted For 5.8.97 738	Copyright Copy 6
Direct Sales Percentage 47%	Copies to Durham Office 24
Discount Sales Percentage 40%	Damaged Copy 1
Retail Book Price £23.25	Copies Dispatched as Orders ..72

It would seem prudent to accept total sales are split as 50 percent direct and 50 percent indirect, this being considered a somewhat normal situation. Let us examine the effect of this, relative to the above:

Computer Printout 1 - Sales Discount- Direct and Indirect Sales:-
Conditions:
        50% direct sales, 50% indirect discounted sales.
        Capital £14,000
        Retail Book Price = £18.00 - Print Run 738
        copies, unaccounted shortfall of 62 copies
        C = £14,000. Ds = 50%
        N = 738 = Sd = 40%
        Rs = £18.00
Total Revenue Rs { (N * 0.5) + Ds * (N * 0.5)}
        = £18 { (738 * 0.5) + 0.6 * (738 * 0.5)]
        = £18 (369 + 221.4)
        = £10,627.2
    Profit Loss:-   **= £10.627.2 - £14,000 = - £3,372.8**

To have accepted a retail book price under these latter circumstances would have involved the author in the loss of £3,373 (which is in opposition to the publisher's stated policy of "Break Even or Small Profit."

    [Note:- 738 copies sold on the basis of 50% & 40 % direct & discounted sales respectively = 591 copies. @ Retail Book Price of £18.00) = £10.638]

In order to secure the Publishers policy of each book achieving break-even point or making a small profit, the only avenue left, with which to ease this situation, would be to increase the book's retail price, as determined below: Taking into account the shortfall of 62 books, together with non-remunerative disposed copy. Effective print run has been reduced from 800 (contract specification) copy to 706 {(800-(62+32)}

Resultant Revised Situation

$$\text{Revised Per Capita Book Price} = \frac{C}{N} = \frac{£14000}{706} = £19.83$$

Breakeven Retail Book Price is now:- = £19.83/0.80=£24.78

This had the effect of adversely affecting the book's competitive capability on the basis of : all things being equal, the lower the retail price, the greater will be the public interest and of market feedback, the agreed book price was compromised at £23.25.

The apparent publisher loss of 62 books further adversely compounds the situation to the disadvantage of the author. I do not think it reasonable to expect the average first edition author to be familiar with or able to, undertake such analyses in normal circumstances, nor should he be required to do so in view of the publisher's publicity stated policy referred to earlier.

It was but fortuitous in this case the situation came to light in the manner it did. It inspired the Author to undertake deep investigations and research into the background circumstances. During the early stages the Publisher being informed of matters relevant to the high book cost, responded:-

"You suggested and agreed the book's retail price level",

hardly a positive approach to the wider situation in which he had failed to give proper attention to the book's retail price fixing in the first instance, which in the event contravened his own policy of breakevenl profit on all first edition publications", and a compromise was the only solution, requests for an increased print run having been turned down.

INCLUSION OF PRODUCTION COST VARIABLE

IN the interests not only of the publisher's own organisational efficiency, but also those projected interests of future submitters of manuscripts, such lapses cannot be dismissed as "no big deal". They need to be explained and eliminated in the natural order of things.

The only value we now require to complete this analysis is that of the actual cost of production and promotion for the second edition. They are not the same. In the former situation many costs of servicing the manuscript to its final finished book format are not to be repeated (other than maybe of updating or modifying the reprint in some manner or other).

However, it need not deter making a calculated approach both with regard to the first and subsequent editions and to this end a computer programme was developed on the basis of the foregoing calculations.

EXPLANATION OF PUBLISHER'S ESTIMATED CAPITAL COSTS

Element	Projected Costs £	Per Capita
Editorial	1,237	1.55
Typesetting	4,062	5.08
Jacket Design & Production	1,234	1.54
Printing & Binding	4.646	5.81
Promotion	1,563	1.95
Administration	1,730	2.16
TOTAL COSTS:	£14,472	£18.09

It will be noted that the above cost breakdown makes no provision for the publisher's profit allocation. Even allowing for the widest degree of generosity in the interpretation of such values, I find them difficult to understand. Of the values quoted, printing and binding appear substantially on the high side. However, total setting-up and overhead costs of some £9,826 (£14,472 - £4,646), would to me, in my former situation, have called for a great deal of "in depth analysis" on each of the elements.

This is a matter of significance to the author, particularly where the publisher states his average capital charge as approximately £6,000, the £14,472 projected being 241% greater.

Relative to a "Second or Edition" assuming an actual total cost of:-

"printing and binding + general overheads + limited additional promotion costs = £7.50"
The effect of 50% Direct Sales with Indirect Sales discounted 40%=(800-640) 160 copies.
The profit on the full disposal of 800-2nd Edition Copy
$$= 640 \times (23.25 - £7.50) = £10,080$$
Publisher's Share @ 85%=£8,568 (it is suggested these percentages are negotiable)

Author's Share @ 15%=£1,512

It will be appreciated that the break-even level shown above, will rise and fall with the changing values of the variants direct sales percentage and discount sales percentage, or indeed any of the variables.

I believe the publisher's estimate of £18 was on the basis of experienced guestimation. It certainly wasn't, in my opinion, determined by analysis or calculation.

The importance of this position lies in the fact that £18 is a far better competitive price than £23.25 within the market place, which is further adversely affected by the addition of the £2 inland and £5.00 overseas mail order charges respectively.

By reason of a publisher's failure to correlate more effectively the three elemental factors of capital charge, print run and retail book price at this stage in the manuscript's processing, the projected book's competitive edge is blunted and penalised, even before a book is printed.

This can arise in two ways: An unscrupulous publisher allocates to himself excessive profit through the capital charge he levies upon the author, or the print run (number of books contracted to be published) is set too low in relation to that capital charge and the resultant retail book price at break-even is thus fixed at a higher level than ought otherwise to have been the case.

Excessively inflating cost projections of various elements to conceal profit allocation, can have the same effect as the factors just outlined. Since these are not disclosed, there is little risk of challenge. Moreover, first-time emerging writers generally have little or no experience in such matters, and certainly have no yardsticks with which to check the authenticity or otherwise of such situations.

COMPUTER AIDED DETERMINATIONS

At this point I decided to research the whole situation in great depth, inclusive of the detail contained in the Publishers 1995 Book Catalogue, developing "computer aids" with which to do so. This was quite an ambitious approach, one which seeks to cover most contingencies likely to be encountered, with the greatest of flexibility, and enable a wide range of interpolations relative to the three elements under discussion to be determined. Quite a variety of computer "spreadsheets" were developed in the light of the calculations above, construction of which is not too difficult, maybe a little laborious, (but worthwhile pursuing where an heavy Capital Outlay such as featured is involved). One such example was of "logarithmic table dimension," the incorporated variables are listed below:-

PRIMARY VARIABLES	SECONDARY DERIVED VARIABLES
1. Author's Capital Charge	1. Indirect Sales Percentage
2. Publisher's Allocated Print Run	2. Indirect Sales - Number of Books.
3. Book's Retail Price	3. Direct Sales - Number of Books
4. Direct Sales Percentage	4. Publisher's Profitability
5. Discount Sales Percentage	5. Author's Profitability
6. Production Costs	6. Print Run
7. Authors Profit Percentage	7. Retail Book Price.
	8. Capital Cost Per Book.

Here manipulation possibilities approach those of an exercise in "campanology". The possibilities are virtually indeterminable. However, the final version developed very simple, powerful and highly flexible–is reproduced herewith: at the end of this chapter.

ANALYSIS OF PUBLISHERS CONTRACT VALUES:

Entering variables from computer keyboard automatically computes all values shown:-
Publishers Capital Charge-cell a3-£14,000
Print Run Range-100 to 1500
Base of print run-cell d3-500
Per Capita Book Prices £28.00 to £9.33
Incremental Print Run Interval-d4-100
Breakeven Prices-£35.00 to £11.67
Direct Sales Percentage-a15-50%
Ceiling Retail Prices-£70.00 to £23.33
Ceiling Retail Prices are taken at "twice the breakeven retail book price" an arbitrary value which can be varied
Discount Percentage:- cell 17 40%
Breakeven Minimum Sales - 200 to 600
Conversion Factor Appropriate to Sales Split & Discount Percentage-0.80

ANALYSIS:- PUBLISHER'S CAPITAL CONTRACT CONDITIONS

	a	b	c	d	e	f	g	h	i	j	k	l	m
Capital	14000												
Range of Print Run		Print Run			500	to	1500	Conversion Factor			0.8		
		Increment		100									
			500	600	700	800	900	1000	1100	1200	1300	1400	1500
Capital Cost Per Book			£28.00	£23.33	£20.00	£17.50	£15.56	£14.00	£12.73	£11.67	£10.77	£10.00	£9.33
Per Book Cost Breakeven		Lower	£30.00	£29.17	£25.00	£21.88	£19.44	£17.50	£15.91	£14.58	£13.46	£12.50	£11.67
Retail Book Price		*Upper	£70.00	£58.33	£50.00	£43.75	£38.89	£35.00	£31.82	£29.17	£26.92	£25.00	£23.33
Breakeven Minima Sales		*	200	240	280	320	360	400	440	480	520	560	600
Direct Sales %	50	0.50											
Indirect Sales	50	0.50											
Sales Discount %	40	0.60											

ELEMENT

Lower Limit–Break even

Upper Limited – 100% Above Breakeven

*Based Upon Upper Limit Value

*Script Values "Exclusively Subject to Change from Keyboard"

Cells – e4,b3,b15 & b17

Retail Price fixed at twice the breakeven Book Price to provide a wide margin for consideration.

You may alter the values of any one combination or all of those variables depicted in "italics" from the keyboard in which case relevant new values to all detail expressed will automatically compute.

This is probably the most useful and versatile of the calculating tools developed hereto and will be helpful to an authors check of the likely effects of a publishers assessment, of capital, print run and book retail prices.

Additional examples are given, from which it will be noted how one can quickly assess a potential situation even if only provided with the Authors Capital Charge. However, other versions have been developed to meet the circumstances of:

1. Where the publisher issues two values, Capital Charge and Print with the retail book price to be determined at a later date, and

2. Where all three values - capital charge, print run - and retail Book prices are given (This is an American example embracing the same contract)

Both are designed to test the potential profitability involved, over-pricing and/or print run shortfalls.

Within the Publishing trade there is a network of communications, designed to inform all "retail outlets" of a new book's release, with provision for alteration upgrading in a systematic manner.

Despite the fact that all the information required and the ISBN had been obtained, and some 12 months "lead time" was available with which the Publisher could have notified these services when the book was to be released–he failed to do so until several weeks after the book appeared in the public domain. The result was that "senior citizen miners and others" of limited means, were unable to obtain a copy through the various nationally recognised retail outlets. To me this represented an important "lapse" one which could be considered as inexcusable in the circumstances. Representations were made to the publisher concerning this. I felt them to have been dismissed as a matter of no great importance.

Where under the conditions of any publishing contract, or joint agreement, between author and a publisher, mutual joint concern with a "books retail price" is paramount–overpricing has the effect of impairing its acceptance by

MEMOIR / AUTOBIOGRAPHY	NUMBER	PAGES	PRICE £'S	PAGES PER BOOK No.
1. SECTION - MEMOIR/AUTOBIOGRAPHY	33	7871	416.133	239
2. SECTION - WAR	15	3227	187.90	215
3. SECTION - SOCIAL HISTORY	9	1696	106.86	188
4. SECTION - HISTORY	6	1746	128.50	291
5. SECTION - SCOTTISH - INTEREST	12	1976	138.80	165
6. SECTION - BIOGRAPHY	6	1381	94.15	230
7. SECTION - MARITIME	6	1591	87.40	265
8. SECTION - SCIENCE & EDUCATION	6	1115	67.96	186
9. SECTION - RELIGION & PHILOSOPHY	15	3287	179.40	219
10. SECTION - TRAVEL	3	626	27.95	209
11. SECTION - POLITICS & ECONOMICS	3	371	21.44	124
12. SECTION - LITERATURE	3	446	33.50	149
13. SECTION - FICTION	18	3808	199.69	212
14. SECTION - CHILDREN'S FICTION	6	389	31.35	65
15. SECTION - POETRY	9	739	55.49	82
	150	30027	1,838.42	2831

2 THE PRIMARY LIST = BROADER DETAIL
PUBLISHER'S 1995 BOOK LIST
MEMOIR & AUTOBIOGRAPHIES

Book No.	Page Size mm	Page Area sq cms	Pages No:-	Price £	Total sq: cms	Page Area Cumulative
1	210 X 148	311	239	14.95	74,281	
2	210 X 148	311	265	13.50	82,362	156,643
3	210 X 148	311	246	12.95	76,457	233,100
4	210 X148	311	271	16.50	84,227	317,327
5	234 X 156	365	220	14.95	80,309	397,636
6	210 X 148	311	207	14.99	64,336	461,971
7	210 X 148	311	298	17.50	92,618	554,590
8	210 X 148	311	209	14.50	64,957	619,5470
9	210 X 148	311	129	10.50	40,093	659,640
10	210 X 148	311	301	16.50	93,551	753,191
11	210 X 148	311	220	15.50	68,376	821,567
12	210 X 148	311	104	10.95	32,323	853,890
13	210 X 148	311	184	14.95	57,187	911,077
14	210 X 148	311	296	15.00	91,997	1,003,074
15	210 X 148	311	228	14.95	70,862	1,073,937
16	210 X 148	311	140	12.50	43,512	1,117,449
17	210 X 148	311	117	8.50	36,364	1,153,812
18	302 X 216	652	133	12.50	86,759	1,240,571
19	210 X 148	311	147	12.50	45,688	1,286,258
20	234 X 156	365	162	18.50	59,136	1,345,395
21	234 X 156	365	478	21.95	78,849	1,424,243
22	210 X 148	311	216	16.50	170,318	1,594,562
23	210 X 148	311	548	24.50	64,957	1,659,519
24	210 X 148	311	69	4.95	21,445	1,680,964
25	210 X 148	311	204	8.99	63,403	1,744,367
26	210 X 148	311	166	13.50	51,593	1,795,960
27	210 X 148	311	264	10.00	82,051	1,878,011
28	234 X 256	311	121	16.50	37,607	1,915,618
29	234 X156	365	581	17.00	212,088	2,127,706
30	210 x148	311	121	13.95	37,607	2,165,313
31	210 X 148	311	171	14.5	53,147	2,218,460
32	234 X156	365	360	16.5	131,414	2,349,874
33	210 X 148	311	214	16.5	66,511	2,416,386
Averages		**329**	**223**	**14.27**	**73,224**	**73,224**

the public, underpricing increases the difficulty of a break-even achievement. In spite of this I feel it to be the lessor of two evils. Here the first-time author is at a distinct disadvantage. More than likely he lacks the basic knowledge with which to make the effort to contribute effectively. (At least that was my situation at the time). The publisher has all the background knowledge of his

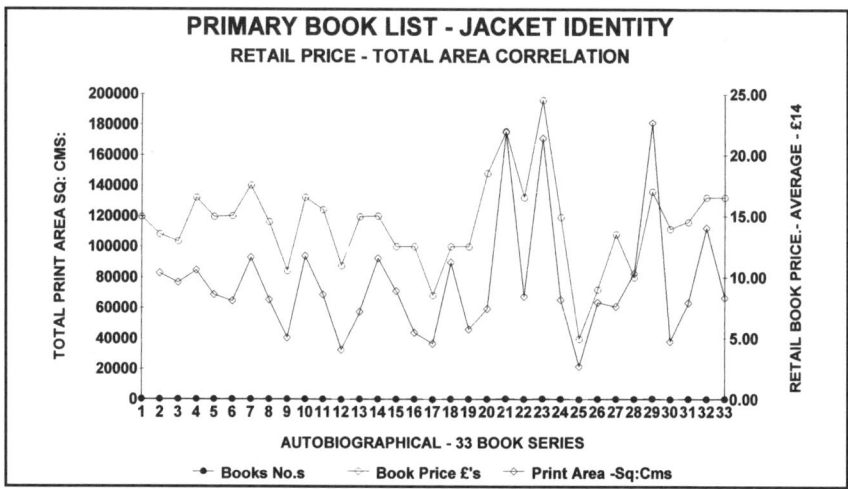

former and current publications and promotional experience to work with. Sporting a hunch is an easy thing to do–but unlike the race-track punter with his losses,–Author's likelihood of a heavy potential "capital loss" is of a greater concern to him.

To offset his difficulties the race-going punter might turn to the Sporting Life or some other racing journal for guidance. Fine! In a like manner "what

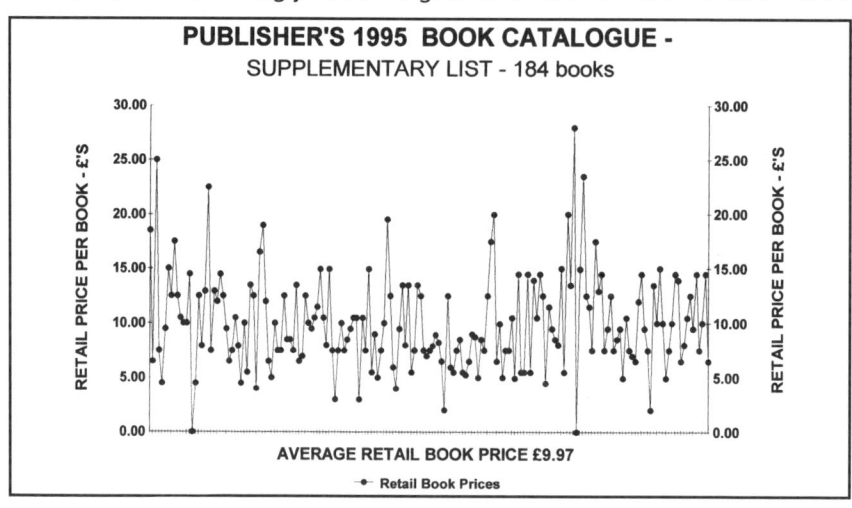

could be better than for the would-be author to turn to the Publisher's most recent issue of his "book list catalogue" for a similar purpose. By reason of the nature of his manuscript, he needs to look for a category of book titles into which his own work will fit. There is not much point in choosing the section on romantic or political novels for a highly specialised work in Crystallography or Greek Mythology!

The nearest category to suit my purpose was that of "Autobiography" and maybe in part "Sociology" or "Industrial & Social History" in which it was felt that, all first time manuscript submissions therein, stood a more equal chance of success when subjected to public exposure. This particular category embodied 33 books of widely different titles and subjective experiences. It may rightly be regarded that a sample of 33 rpm a total of 334 or 10 per cent is low–but, for my purpose of attempting to understand what publishing was all about, the sample proved quite useful. This sample was examined in terms of book size, page content, total print area and book retailing selling price–all of which are embodied in the statistical tables which follow. Before proceeding to outline the work undertaken and the matters to be revealed in connection therein, let me first sketch in a few basics.

1. The Primary List–Main titles:- embraces 15 categories–having jacket illustrated reference and broader detail of each book featured therein–refers to some 150 titles.

PUBLISHER'S SECTIONALISED 1995 BOOK LIST

The section Memoirs and autobiographies attracted 33 manuscripts, followed by the section Fiction with 18 accepted submissions in 2nd place with the sections, War and Religion and Philosophy in joint 3rd place.

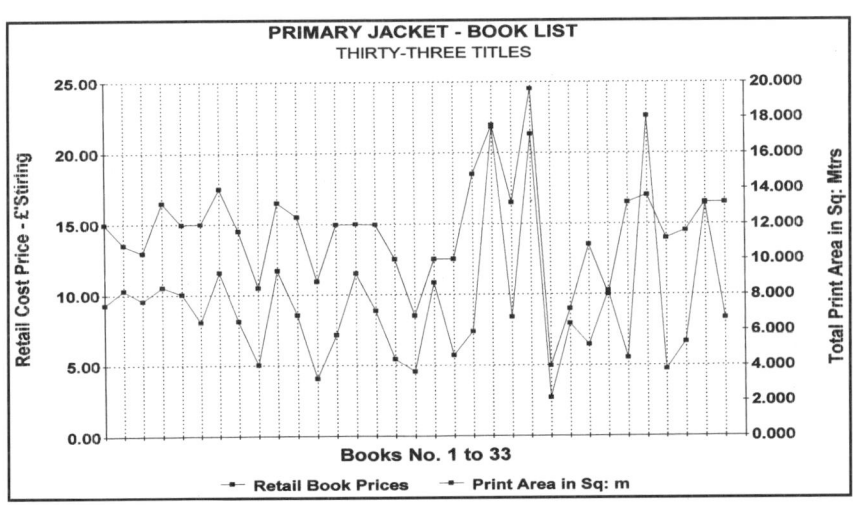

AUTOBIOGRAPHICAL SECTION

This publishers list embraces the basic detail of each book in terms of title, author, price and IBSN identification, book sizes, total print area, and cumulative print area.

My first impressions, on reading the chart, were that an apparent degree of symmetric relationship prevailed with the first half of the books examined, whereas with the section of books on the right-hand side the situation has changed quite dramatically – maybe random fixed price charges having no mathematical of logical background relationship. How far the greater spread of high priced books – £16 to £20 – contributed to this in terms of overcharging is a matter for deeper and further analysis.

Primary & Supplementary Situation: Book Retail Prices

Books - 150 Total Cost = £1,784 - Average Book Price £11.89
Books - 184 Total Cost = £1,834.35 - Average Book £ 9.97
Books - 334 Total Cost = £3,618.82 - Average Book £10.83

The Supplementary Lists - Other Titles. Book Lists

Chart Supplementary List -

This chart is an alternative form of presentation to the one above – and provides the similar information.

DETERMINATION OF "PRINT RUN" AVERAGE

In the circumstances developed above, to determine the average print run for all contracts being serviced by the publisher, it would be necessary to have access all printed and bound book delivery invoices pertaining to each individually signed contract. Reference has been made to the fact that the print run contract specified is not necessarily the same as that which is physically produced and delivered. In relation to contract specification, in my own case in the event the publisher's "book balance" the "opening stock" was 738 – a shortfall of 62 copies, which at £17.50 per capita book charge works out at a further loss of £1,085.00 .

As matters have worked out, my situation has been fortuitous. Had it not been for my solicitor's advice to take over the book stock from the publisher, I believe such information would never have surfaced.

What I found to be truly disconcerting, onerous and highly disturbing was to discover how little control an author retains over his personal assets. Once he contracts a publisher to service them, he receives no information in the manner with which the publisher manipulates them with respect to his contact with outside agencies. Useful detail and transaction are not made available to him, nor is he consulted or informed in such matters. He receives no systematic reports as to how matters are progressing. He is virtually impotent. Only in the final analysis is he able to exert any real authority, by withdrawing those assets in converted book format – not without loss and great discomfort through problems of keeping and storing stock.

It can be argued, and is indeed true that an author is free to accept or reject a contract in any manner he chooses. Maybe that is so, but if what has been experienced I believe, is that Vanity Press and Subsidised Publishing operate contracts that are not even handed and are heavily biased in the Publisher's favour.

The publisher exercises his sole power to fix the print run without reference to or consultation with the author. This is an abuse of the circumstances prevailing, and creates all sorts of problems leading to exploitation, book over-pricing, diminished promotional prospects, heavier per capita capitalisation costs, and greater potential losses to an author.

Two actual cases A and B below are considered relative to this, the basic features being as tabulated in the following:

	A	B	Remarks
Book Size & Quality -	Identical	Identical	Same Publisher
Pages	400+	399	Fixed by Publisher
Capital Charge	£7,000	£14,000	Fixed by Publisher
Print Run	300	800	Fixed by Publisher
Book Retail Price	£10.00	£18.00	Fixed by Publisher

Now let us analyse the publisher's projected situation a stage further. He has actually set the course for the author's to sustain a minimum loss of £4,600 and £3,373.00 respectively on the total disposal of his 300 and 800 books., irrespective of unsold copies or remainders. In the circumstances relating to the first break even the "retail book price" is determined as:-

Per Capita Book Cost = Capital Charge / Print Run. = £7,000/300
= £23.33

Break-even book price = £23.33/0.80 (Note: 0.8 is the factor which takes care of the sales split and discount rates of 50 and 40 percent)
= £29.17

At such a price the book particularly as being a "novel" by a unknown author is substantially dammed before it hits the book stands. This is particularly so when copies of the leading author's works can be obtained substantially below the price.

a) As the "per capita cost" of the book increases the author is progressively penalised, either by the effects of overpricing and/or greater subsidies to the retailer, and no doubt the publisher, the latter for the reasons discussed hereto. Consider the following situation:-

"book fairly engineered to give an author and publisher a fair percentage profit of say 20% with direct mailing. Along comes the big retailer–taking a 40% cut based on the "book's production cost+20% profit". The 20% difference has to come from somewhere. It does, a subsidy from the profit made on authors' direct sales."

Such a situation can leave both the publisher and retailer with profit whilst the author sustains a heavy loss. This point is developed later in the book.

Consider a printer quotation below, regarding the influence of getting the "print run right."

b) Book A5 size-Price includes basic layout, typesetting, and reproduction, cover design and artwork, any scanning and redrawing of graphs, charts and graphics with 4 colour cover:-

Number of copies-1,000 £4,700.   2,000 copies £5,300
Per Capita Book Price = £4.70   Per Capita Book Price - £2.65

This shows how the "per capita cost" of a book falls dramatically with an increase of print run–thus providing substantial room for manoeuvre in the overall scheme of things.

c) Examination of "Remaindered" Aspects, with copy sold up to the first 300–the author's situation is unchanged, is left with a minimum loss of £4,600 which he can't recover. With the revised approach each copy sold in excess of 300 (with greatly reduced retail book prices the prospects for this are better) reduces his potential losses.

How often, why, and for what purpose does the publisher project financial losses on his authors in the manner outlined? These are fair considerations to be addressed. In relation to his promises and expressed policy.

Could it be failure on the Marketing side–indirectly enhance and maximises his profits on the production site–by reducing time and effort involved therein, hence likely disinterest in a book's promotion once a manuscript emerges as a finished book?

Putting a generous side to one's thinking, might it not be pure incompetence, where a publisher's potential assessments lead to a financial loss to the author before a book is printed? Only the publisher knows the true situation.

Whilst great stress has been directed towards price fixing, there will always be a problem of remaindered books, (i.e. unsold stock–after the "tenure of the contract has terminated), in which the lock stock and barrel are brought up at nominal prices–and disposed thereafter through bookstores and super-stores at heavily discounted prices (for which the authors receive no compensation). This need not necessarily be a bad thing from a public spirited point of view in that it enables people to buy copy which they could not afford, or would not buy in other circumstances.

In that readers are particularly fussy with regard to the works they read, there will always be situations which are exclusive for some valid reason or other. However I again repeat the volume of sales is very dependent upon the cover prices, because books are discretionary purchases. Price is more an issue for direct sales, than for indirect sales, hence the need to consider in the latter case–the total costs of copy i.e. book retail price + package and posting, keeping that as low as possible to attract the greatest public possible attention.

Again, the conclusion is that demand is a variable influenced by the publisher. It should not be assumed that demand will exceed the size of the initial run, at whatever level this is fixed.

The dynamics of the relationship between author and publisher differ greatly between private and commercial publishing. In private publishing the publisher is merely a technical agent, servicing without financial risk to himself the author's attempts to have his manuscript published and promoted within the public arena as a saleable commodity. In commercial publishing, the publisher is much more exposed, and must make larger profits on the successes to compensate for the failures. Commercial publishers are less likely to accept a work for a publication if the best outcome is a small profit, but are under more financial pressure to promote, with vigour, the books they do accept. Another difference is the acceptable speed of sales – a situation in which a "commercial publisher" cannot afford to maintain a large stock of a title that sells slowly.

In academic publishing it is accepted that the minimum economic print run is 1,500 copies, which must be sold in three selling seasons. The book is physically produced in July or August for the pending academic year, and any unsold stock dumped some 27 months later. In private publishing the author may be more willing to have his capital tied up for much longer. Recently I was informed that some publishers' accountants are even more ruthless by dumping unsold stock little more than 12 months after publication.

To end this section I can do no better than quote verbatim from a most helpful and encouraging letter dated January 2nd, 1997, I received from Mr Ron Adams – husband of Lynne Adams, the lady who started me out on the adventures recounted hereto and to follow, one which has had tremendous advantageous repercussions both with regard to my physical and mental well being, and pleasure in retirement–to whom I express my grateful thanks.

"You must have long realised, Charles, that writing a serious book is, like having a child, a total disaster if you take an accountant's view, and put a price on the time expended. You obviously had great fun

in writing Machinations In Coal-mining and can take satisfaction at repaying a debt that every man owes to his profession. A younger man with family commitments could not have afforded that book . Perhaps the most valuable message you can pass onto others derives from your age, and has nothing to do with money at all."

How neatly and succinctly he has summed up my situation, particularly in view of the fact that he has had wide experience within the publishing industry, part of which has been helpfully recorded herein and which is so acknowledged with grateful thanks. However such sentiments are not to be heeded any way as "justifiable countenance" to those involved in what might be considered as "nefarious practices motivated by dishonesty and greed" in the exploitation of their fellow-humans trying to contribute their offerings to the world at large.

MY OWN SALES PROMOTIONS

When the books arrived from the publisher I felt, quite strangely, fully at ease with the situation. My mind was settled and I had accepted the fact that recovering all, or even a fair percentage, of the £14,000 capital charge I had outlayed had not the slightest chance of being achieved. At that point, although I had thought a great deal about the problems likely to be faced, I had no clear determined line of action mapped out.

I had developed no ill feelings other than occasional emotional anger being engendered from time to time, but that had been normal to me in the former exacting career in which I had been raised. Such emotions had always proved to be transient, only to disappear completely within a short time, never to become permanently lasting. In fact I have throughout my life schooled myself in the philosophy that whatever adversities one has to meet, by adopting a positive approach towards the matters in hand, or by looking beyond the difficulties, cancerous thought with its destructive effect upon one's intellectual and imaginative processes and ideas, stands little chance of taking a hold of and corrupting character.

However, one facet in the whole situation stood out clearly with the intensity of penetrating beams from a lighthouse on the darkest of nights. I had, as Ron Adams has stated, successfully accomplished an act which the young adult with his growing family could scarcely hope to emulate for many sound reasons. What to me was also of great importance was that I had put something back into this great mining industry of ours in recompense for the rewards I and my family had received from it.

Undaunted and with enthusiasm refreshed, letters were sent out seeking to retain the former retail outlets, honouring the terms and conditions previously established with the publisher. Further to such action, notices in the form of letters were sent out to the media who had been previously been contacted with reference to reviews. The object was to advise of the changed and new circumstances

Contact with Whitakers Bibliographic Services with the object of getting re-established on the retail trade communication channels was made, a situation in which the service was most helpful.

A further approach to the television and news media was set in motion. Two examples follow – the first to technical journals, the second to the normal press, radio, television and other media.

My first letter was to the editor of Mining Technology, (the official journal of the Institution of Mining Engineers). I was a member of this organisation for well over 50 years. The editor was most kind and helpful:

From CHARLES ROUND. C.ENG: F.I.M.E.. Telephone (01823) 256794 10 Lavender Grove Bishops Hull Taunton Somerset TA1 5QA
To: Dr G.J.M. Woodrow. Editor Mining Technology, The Institution of Mining Engineers, Danum House, South Parade, Doncaster, South Yorkshire.
9th July 1997

Dear Editor,
              "Machinations in Coal-mining"
Please accept my beholden thanks for your kindness in accepting and publishing Mr Trevor Massey's review of the above book in the May 1997 issue of Mining Technology.
I would also publicly thank both Mr Trevor Massey. OBE, BSc (Hons) C.Eng: F.I.M.E. and Dr Gordon Fatkin for their kind favours in under-taking the work of reviewing the book on behalf of Mining Technology and Minerals Industry International respectively – their reviews were beneficent and inspiring to me. They have my eternal gratitude.
To my former esteemed colleagues, friends and all those who have written to me, please accept my heartfelt thanks. Even at this late stage in a very long mining career, such contributions strengthen my love for our great and noble industry.
No matter one's circumstances I honestly believe we all owe the Industry a great deal, and whatever can be ploughed back to enhance its image is worthy of the effort.
To all those who had difficulty in obtaining copy in the early stages of the book's publication, please accept my apologies. Having taken custody of all remaining copies future enquiries will be processed from the above address. Discussions and consultation with the book retail outlets are currently being undertaken.
Following recent discussions at the International Mining Exhibition – 4th and 5th June 1997 at the Doncaster Exhibition Centre – with many retired colleagues, mining engineers, young students , Selby miners and others, consideration has been given to the mail order price. This has been rebated from £23.25 + £2.00) = £25.25 total, down to £18.50 + £1.45 (packing & postage) in the hope it will be come more accessible to a wider audience, for more people to enjoy.
     Your sincerely
     Charles Round

The publication of this letter was most inspiring. Acquaintances with a number of old friends and colleagues were re-established and new ones created. There was also a secondary and important development arising from this publication. It established contact with the Cefn Coed Colliery Museum, located at Crynant, Neath, West Wales, through Mr C.W. Rees, a member of its staff.

This museum, a converted old mine, is run by the Neath Port Talbot County Borough Council, and during the period 1960-1965 it operated as a mine under my direction. At the time I was area general manager in charge of the S.W. Division's No.9 (Neath) Area anthracite coalfield.

Mr Rees, or Chris as I knew him (his father had been an official at Abernant Colliery during my period of service in the area), following receipt of a copy of Machinations in Coal-mining, was greatly impressed. He placed orders for an additional five copies, and with an act of great kindness and generosity contacted Mr Dennis Parkhouse, closely associated with the family publishers The Archive Shop, 47-49 High Street, Lydney, Gloucestershire GL15 5DD. This address serves also as the editorial address for the Lightmoor Press. The proprietors, as publishers and booksellers Neil and Heather Parkhouse (with the support of Neil's father Dennis Parkhouse) specialise in industrial and transport history.

I was contacted by Mr Dennis Parkhouse and a meeting was arranged with, the publishers, at their business address, for Wednesday December 17, 1997. The meeting was held in an excellent atmosphere. It was obvious to me the publisher, Neil, and his father, Dennis Parkhouse, were both skilled persons, knowledgeable of the publishing trade at great depth, and had great enthusiasm for the work they were doing. Discussions centred round the current book's promotion, and what help they were prepared to give in that direction. It was agreed that the book would be promoted in the March edition of their publication Archive. They had received an excellent review, highly supportive of their own views and impressions, from a completely independent authority. What gave my accompanying friend and colleague Derek Irwin and I great confidence was the honesty of purpose. Derek throughout has been to me a proverbial tower of strength. His consideration for my advanced age, together with his unstinted great practical support to that end, has been no less than that of a son offering great encouragement – no matter the circumstances.

The Publisher's failure to inform the Whitaker Bibliographical Services to the Book Trade's Retail Outlets, of the Book's emergence as a published title, despite over one years available "lead" time with which to do so, gives rise to speculative thinking such as–inefficient management or–management failings, low level of operational efficiency, promotional disinterest, complete disregard for authors interests having received his full profit allocation.

The effects upon some of the leading chain-books-sellers, book warehouses, and the trade generally are indicated by the following order processing dates:-

BOOK PUBLISHED - COMPLIMENTARY ADVANCE COPY
16TH DECEMBER 1996
RETAIL BOOK DISPOSALS – EARLY ORDERS

Brendon Books..............................03.03.97 - First Order
Scarthin Books 20.03.97
E. Garland & Sons..........................22.05.97
Austicks Books & Music 29.05.97
Gardners Books ....06.06.97 - First Order
Barnsley Bookshop........................01.07.97
W.H. Smith 10.07.97
Boytes Unifoyle Ltd 10.07.97
Lindsay & Howes 31.07.97
James Askew & Sons ....13.08.97 - First Order

I have long felt that providence or fate is never unmindful of the difficulties and problems which beset we humans, and tries to redress any imbalance, or give us the strength from time to time to push on regardless when we meet difficult times. This meeting I felt to be another example in a long chain of many such redresses.

One major lesson that I have learned, from what has hereto been but limited contact from these people, is that great emphasis is laid upon pre-advertising a title before it appears in print. – three months in advance at least can be the accepted practice.

Contrast this with my experience so far, in which, for a period of up to three months after the book was released, the retail trade was generally unaware of its existence.

Reflecting on this brought back practical memories of an early experience, recorded in detail in the book which has given rise to the matters now being narrated. In 1983 I became involved in trying to establish a series of Heritage in Brass recordings by converting old 78rpm records of the St Hilda Colliery Brass Band (1869-1937, Durham Coalfield) under its celebrated musical director, James Oliver, to the then more popular LP 33rpm format. Forward notices some eight months before the contracted release date were issued to the whole of the brass band world. The response of the old bandsmen and professional musicians was tremendous, so much so that I virtually had accrued sufficient forward subscriptions to cover the cost of a second recording, which at the time had not been envisaged.

Deciding to go ahead with the second recording, I chose to feature the early virtuoso trumpet player Jack Macintosh (1891 - 1979) playing 18 popular ballads, operatic arias and celebrated "virtuosi solo" compositions. Some 2,000 (1,000 in each case) were produced and received with great acclaim from the old world brass bandsmen.

This was a lesson within my own experience of the value of forward publicity.

The second letter standard copy (here addressed to the Times Supplement) was sent to all previous sources which were covered on the publisher's original media distribution list:

Review Editor, The Times Literary Supplement
Admiral House
66-66 East Smithfield
London E1XY Date 9th July 1997

Dear Editor,

"MACHINATIONS IN COAL MINING
ISBN 1-85821-403-3

A few weeks ago I understand you were kindly asked by the publisher to kindly review the above title.

In the meantime there has been a change of circumstance which I would like to advise you of. The reviews and comments I have received from the technical press and the members of the public have been most inspiring and highly rewarding for the two years of continuous effort applied by an octogenarian. Two reviews are attached, one from a highly qualified technician and the other from an old retired miner.

Having taken over custody of the remaining stock of books and set up promotional facilities at the above address, I wanted to inform you of the situation and the fact of having revised the retail price and mail order price of the book as below:

Formerly:- Retail Price:- £23.25. Direct Mail Order Sales - £23.25 + £2.00 - total £25.25

Revised Current:- Retail Price:- £18.50. Direct Mail Order Sales - £18.50 + £1.45 - £19.95

I would like the book to be considered my personal tribute to a great and noble Industry and an acknowledgment to the men and management that made it so. I have tried to produce something of heritage quality for current and former mineworkers (indeed other workers also) for family retention. I hope I have succeeded.

However, as before, there was no response from any source. Maybe I was somewhat naive, and/or over-zealously ambitious, in what really on reflection amounts to seeking gratis publicity and advertising from within the U.K's most powerful sources. The points about reviewing made earlier relative to this are still applicable, however.

Now I would like to continue outlining the book promotional efforts undertaken before and after my continued association with the Archive Book Publishing people.

PROMOTION PACKAGE PREPARATION

IN that the book had, and has, among other attributes, strong social, political, practical and technological mining and other historic interests, my first thoughts were "to what authority and in what direction should my initial efforts be directed?" Also what manner of promotional package would best meet any such determined situation?

The answer virtually leapt onto the computer keyboard: Libraries!

As a permanent repository of community knowledge, information and location for the process of learning, the library has effectively been in existence since the year 300 BC. That age embraced the great Library of Alexandria in Egypt, one of the recognised Seven Wonders of the Ancient World in which more than 500,000 scrolls are said to have been deposited prior to its demise.

The promotional package format did not come so easily, however, in that librarians are motivated on a much higher moral plane than the mere pursuit of profit. Their approach to a book's value can be expected to be different from that of the bookstores and retail outlets. This was the reasoning behind the promotional format adopted:

1. A personal letter of explanation.
2. A reviewer's report.
3. Observations on the book's background and content.

In direct contrast to the publisher's approach of directing his strictly limited promotional publicity efforts to the local Somerset towns, the villages centred on Taunton area and on the Greater London Area, it was felt the former, and indeed current remnant mining areas of South and West Yorkshire, East and South Midlands, Derbyshire, Tyneside and Teeside, Durham and Northumberland had better prospects to offer in terms of wider public interest. After all, these areas for many decades were densely populated by mining communities embracing countless generations of miners and their families. There had been no former joint discussions or consultations with the publisher relative to so-called promotion strategy.

In the BT Telephone Service Yellow Pages directories relevant to the defined mining localities above, over 350 city, town and village libraries were targeted and promotional packages prepared, duplicated, assembled, and addressed for and to the Chief Librarian – a labour of some 10 days of about 10 hours' daily duration.

A rough estimate of the total cost of this exercise, inclusive of office materials, computer consumables, external duplication and postal charges can be put at over £300. The sales arising there from are listed later. In his contract estimates the publisher states he allocated £1,563 or $ 2,532 for the book's promotion within the "capital charges" he fixed.

From the evidence in promotional terms produced hereto and in the absence of advice or detail, I would find it difficult to accept other than but a small amount had been spent, chiefly on postage. With regard to promotional effort as stated I felt very strongly about the projection of book detail on the American Market, in which a strategically selected list of 300 engineers and associates out of an estimated 20/30,000 SME members to be targeted, had been prepared by myself.

However the publisher would not honour what was formerly agreed with his representative at the contract signing. Later, under pressure, he claimed he wanted to test the UK market before making a commitment,

What is important in the situation was that such a concept, not previously discussed or referred to me, had been applied to the UK Market. This I subsequently tested by random enquiries to determine whether or not any of the 250 UK persons I had formerly listed had received mail order solicitation. The sample of eight was too small, but the result does indicate the possibility exists . The result was inconclusive – two persons had received copies, one was unsure, two had not, and three persons did not reply.

The sad thing about a situation of this kind is that when faith and confidence breaks down between two contracting parties the fallout can be both unwarranted and unpleasant, particularly in circumstances of entrenchment by either or both of the parties concerned. At a point such as this a sense of realism in terms of involvement really does become deeply manifest.

With the type of contract under consideration, as I reason the position, the publisher acts as an agent, servicing an author's desire to have his manuscript processed, published and promoted as a conventional book, with the author responsible for the financing of the full service specified and taking the major portion of the risk.

The situations under which the publisher takes financial risk include:

1) Where he fails to assess the true nature and cost of that service he seeks to provide. In such circumstances, although he has freedom to manipulate his projected elemental costs to circumvent or reduce probable financial deficit, (for example spend less on scheduled activities where applicable), it is generally a situation in which he cannot be held to account in the management of the author's capital.

2) Where circumstances arise which subject him to unsuccessful litigation and awards are made in favour of the plaintiff. With non-established writers seeking to achieve their first publication I consider the risk to be but very small. In the long-term he could of course be subject to censure from would-be writers and authors withholding their manuscripts and seeking alternative publishers in situations of bad publicity.

Whether a book succeeds or fails in attracting the public's attention as a fortuitous venture need not necessarily be of anxiety to him, in that in normal circumstances his service has proved to have been profitable immediately the author's last instalment on his capital charge has been met.

The relationships which develop between publisher and author as outlined are quite different to those I experienced between management and mining contractors during my career in the mining industry. They do not become so close, with the author it would seem being tolerated until the book is printed and the next would-be writer comes along. Humoured as with children when it suits, or bulldozed as the case may be in other situations. As with normal day to day transactions in other fields generally, the customer is never wrong. Here the publisher is always right, experience would seem to indicate.

NATURE OF PROMOTIONAL ACTIVITY UNDERTAKEN

Effectively the book was physically available following the 1996 Christmas period. Apart from the material in the promotion document mentioned above that was received before the printed books were delivered on December 16, 1996, I was unaware, other than the promotional strategy, of any proposals as to the nature and conduct the actual promotion was to follow. So far as my awareness was and is concerned, there appears to have been no sort of conventional launching or booksigning ceremony.

It was felt that the title had just drifted onto the book market. I just don't know, but having observed such ceremonies with commercial writers on television, the situation was thought to be odd from a publicity aspect. Maybe that is the way matters of this kind are done at these lower levels within the publishing industry? I repeat, I just don't know – but what I do know from experience in my former career in the coal industry is that when one is about to undertake a project, the greater the impact one can create upon all the participants, the greater the support one will receive from all involved. There just seems to be good publicity generally in public ceremonies of any kind, whatever the circumstances.

ACTIVITIES UNDERTAKEN BY AUTHOR
In the early stages prior to the book's emergence in it's final printed form, advance notices were prepared and circulated to a number of old friends and colleagues whom it was known could be interested.

These advance notices took the form of appraisals and created great interest among them, following which I received many telephone calls over some four or five months asking for details of progress relative to publication. Later, when the book was actually in print, with the help of some of these colleagues approaches were made to the local press in the South Yorkshire and Somerset areas.

In this respect George Smales Beedan, the younger brother of one of my former colliery managers, Maurice Beedan, became and still is a tower of strength in creating and developing interest in the book.

As a boy of about 15 in 1947 George was working in the Elsecar Main Colliery steel-girder straightening shop. At the time that, as colliery manager, I was involved in the design and development of steel supports for use at the coal face. Tthe lad was quite keen and deeply interested in what was taking place.

Drawing him aside I advised him to undertake night school studies with the object of obtaining some kind of career qualifications. Placing him under the direction of the then colliery training officer for help and guidance, I left him to make his own decision. I do not recall making any further contact with him. Moreover, during the many years that have passed since the original contact was made, I do not remember how his situation developed.

Shortly after my book was released I received from the publisher a glowing account of his reactions to the book, following which he made telephone contact, and on his own initiative threw himself enthusiastically into the book's promotion. He was and is greatly supportive, for which I am grateful. However the point is that only recently did I learn that over many years

George had applied himself with the same degree of industry as I had done many years earlier, and had obtained scholarships, successfully graduating through university in engineering subjects.

Later he became one of the leading Dinnington Technical College (South Yorkshire) Lecturers. This is one of the nice things in life one likes to recall. George did much to obtain the interest of the South Yorkshire local press, while I followed up with the press here in Somerset. The two featured references herewith were taken from the Somerset and Doncaster local gazettes. Currently we are now together working on a revised approach to the book's promotion in lieu of the disappointments experienced to this point.

BOOK PURCHASING PROBLEMS

Towards the middle of January 1997, letters and telephone complaints were addressed to me privately indicating there were difficulties in obtaining copies through the publishing industry's major retail outlets in Derby, Sheffield, Stockton-on-Tees, Darlington, Durham. Barnsley. Rotherham and Blackpool.

Updated details of the book, had not been provided by the publisher to Whitaker Contact Bibliographic Services, the main circulating authority for book identification and inclusion on the appropriate national main booksellers' networks. This situation of protracted difficulty in obtaining copies through the retail outlets persisted for a number of weeks. This failure had come about despite the availability of a lead time of upwards of 12 months in which the publisher could have supplied the requisite available information to the said services.

● AUTOBIOGRAPHY IS BURSTING AT THE SEAMS WITH FACTS

Charles' book is a mine of information

□ A FASCINATING story of one man's rise through the ranks of the coal industry, from pit pony driver to national troubleshooter for the coal board, is told by 82-year old Charles Round, of Taunton, in his just published autobiography.

Entitled *Machinations in Coal Mining*, it tells a straightforward story of his life, work and personal achievements. But it is also a very valuable historical work concerning coal mining, packed with a wealth of interesting detail.

The mechanics and machines needed for modern mining are described, the National Coal Board's successes and failures are detailed, and miners at the coal face or in the boardroom are featured.

It seems that everything and everybody is in the book, from Aberfan to Arthur Scargill.

Working life

Mr Round, of Lavender Grove, is a widower with a son and daughter. He was in the coal industry all his working life and when he retired from the coal board went into consultancy, working in America and Spain.

"I find great satisfaction in the fact that the book is considered to be of wide interest to the general public in addition to the mining profession" he said.

He took two years writing the 400-page book which has nearly 100 illustrations. The book is published by The Pentland Press Ltd, Hutton Close, South Church, Bishop Auckland, Durham.

□ LEFT: Author Charles Round — his book covers everything from Aberfan to Arthur Scargill. *Staff photograph*

Book looks back over 60 years of mining

Miner who made it to the top reflects on his life

by Helen Johnston

A FORMER miner who started his working life at 14 as a pony driver underground and rose to become a deputy director has written a book about his career.

Charles Round, now 83 and originally from the Doncaster area, worked at pits all over the country including Tankersley, Rotherham, Barnsley and Hemsworth.

He said: "I've based the book on my own working experiences and have written it for the ordinary miner and miners' families. It's a record of their experiences as well as mine and covers the past 60 years through all the developments, problems and politics."

Mining

After working in Nottingham and Wales, Mr Round returned to Rotherham as area general manager and then went on to Barnsley as deputy director of mining. He also worked at Riddings Colliery in 1970 when the pit was producing 10 tonnes a man compared to the national average of two tonnes.

Mr Round, who now lives near Taunton in Somerset, retired at 58 but was still involved in mining on a consultancy basis, working abroad in America and Spain.

He said: "I got the idea for the book when I was on a flight to New York and got chatting to the lady sitting next to me. She asked me about my work as a miner and when we landed she suggested I write it all down."

Widower Mr Round has two children, four grandchildren and two great-grandchildren. His book is called Machinations in Coal Mining and contains more than 90 photos. Priced at £23.25 it is published by Bantam Press.

93

This was quite a disappointment at the time and frustrating to those involved. Following inquiries on this matter to the publisher, the response was felt to be quite off-handed – a matter of no great import, it seemed. However, I regarded this failure alongside the former ones to meet two specified defaults in publishing dates. Book sales were lost, both here and within the United States. Progress towards resolving the American mail order problem had made no progress, leading me to seek advice from one of the UK's leading consumer protection organisations, Which'?, and its legal department. I had neither desire or intent to pursue the situation through formal legal channels.

With problems of this nature, if the basic cause is not resolved in its early stages, escalation takes place and the situation starts to gain a momentum of it's own, creating a wastage of time, money and effort. Neither party can generally escape some degree of criticism when this arises. Moreover, the lack and difficulty of face to face discussion and direct consultation creates a situation in which correspondence then assumes the main avenue of expression, in which obstinacy, entrenchment arrogance and intense frustration develop. Thus the coinage of honest and fair expression becomes debased, being replaced by misunderstanding, distortion, grave doubts and suspicion. to the detriment of all concerned.

Personally I believe (on the bedrock experience of very many years of joint negotiation relative to materials supply, engineering contracts, and wage negotiations) there is no real substitute for direct discussion and negotiation, although, in the circumstances outlined, these were not encouraged and even considered to be unnecessary,

For anybody who may become involved in any such situations in relation to contract disputes or operational problems, later in this work some of the legal issues are explained.

As I have stated earlier response to the first promotional letter was most encouraging in that it re-established contacts with old and former colleagues of many years standing. The encouragement received from them was highly stimulating and supportive. The second letter to the media, as with former ones sent out by the publisher, elicited no replies.

At this point, lacking experience in the publishing fields of book promotion, having no guidance, and no contacts, the situation was both exacting and gravely uncertain, and no less disconcerting! Negative thoughts crossing my mind were difficult to control. Fortunately for me, however, in my former career I had met many such situations in one form or another - and had established no matter how "bleak" a situation appeared to be, there was always a way forward, so long as one's confidence was not destroyed. The prevailing impasse had to be overcome and as such the challenge was undertaken and things set in motion.

Firstly a sort of business credibility was established in the form of a post box allocation number by an approach to the postal authorities.

I was later allocated the business address:

Post Box No.467
Taunton TA1 5YX
Somerset
United Kingdom.
- a useful approach to start out with.

A second fax telephone line was installed by BT, an administrative pro-for-mat was devised and prepared and a close liaison was established with George Smales Beedan of Wombwell, Barnsley, South Yorkshire.

The next step was to create a format for promotional material, designed to create a recipient's interest in what is being promoted. Circulation of the material was the next important consideration - in this respect as a first approach the chief librarians of South Yorkshire and Nottinghamshire. Local libraries were the sources contacted. Some 300 points of contact were established towards the end of September 1997. It is rather early at the moment to try and assess the effectiveness of this first effort, although early indications are disappointing.

Having accepted and taken the responsibility of promoting the book. (although the signed contract has not been formerly rescinded), my thoughts turned to the American mail order list, the source of my basic troubles with the publisher,

Having prepared a projected American mail order information package and calculated its cost over the 300 points of impact envisaged, I gave considerable thought to the possibility of more effective alternatives. Was this the best way of trying to get the maximum publicity I was looking for in the circumstances?

Through the list I was to achieve direct contact with 300 recipients – a fair percentage of whom might consider it to be junk mail, relegating it to the trash bin without attempting to examine the package contents. Surely there had to be a better and more effective way? Perhaps taking out an advertisement in a well known American mining magazine, Coal Age, was worth considering as an alternative? Of course !

I redrafted the whole of the material towards the end of making an impact within an advertising space of some 16 square inches to solicit mail orders.

Coal Magazine was being sent to me monthly by my old American friend and colleague Irvin Spotte (former president of the Pittston Coal Company – the third largest deep mine coal producer in its time)for over 40 years. I was able to analyse the possibilities and costs carefully before undertaking any approach.

I gave considerable thought to the *"advertisement format"* both in terms of the book's content and also with regard to presentation. The receipt of more than 30 letters of highly favourable comment from readers widely geographically spaced encouraged this latter approach.

The next thing was to work out the projected space and costs involved. from the magazine's classified display costs.

Coal Age - 1997 Classified Advertising 1997
Rates Per Column Inch for Each Insertion.

Per Inch	1 x	3 x	6 x	12 x
Display Classified	$90	$86	$78	$75

Blind Box $25 per insertion
Colour $100 per insertion
(standard blue, green, yellow or red).

For an advertising space" of 4 inch columnar depth over two adjacent columns it will be noted the advertising cost of the book is estimated to be $667 (£400). In the event the actual cost fixed by the publisher was $700 or £414.20 (the exchange rate at the time was running at approximately $1.69 to the £1.00), .to be spread over 20,000 recipients as against the projected 300. Moreover, the time factor in undertaking the work was less than a day compared with up to six days as originally envisaged. The magazine publisher was notified of the desire to place an advertisement accordingly, and this was accepted. The situation was later undertaken by "fax" communication to *"Coal Age"* offices in **Chicago, USA** and cleared within 24 hours–a facsimile is reproduced herewith:-

ADVERTISEMENT PLACED IN "COAL AGE"–USA MINING JOURNAL VOLUME 102–No.12 1997

In the event this approach failed miserably – only two books were sold.

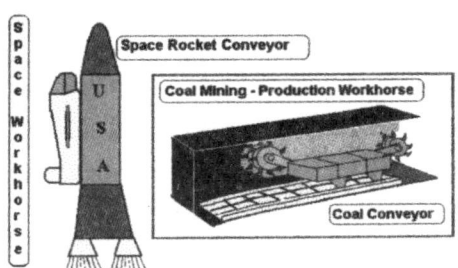

SPACE AGE - MINING TECHNOLOGY

MACHINATIONS IN COAL MINING
BY
CHARLES ROUND. C.ENG. F.I.M.E.

A USEFUL HERITAGE BOOK FOR ALL MINERS
MINING & OTHER COMMUNITIES.
A book of wide historical mining, social, political, psychological,
philosophical and autobiographical interest, to a wide variety of
specialists, management, students and general readers.

ISBN - 1-85827-403-3 - 399 Pages - 95 Illustrations
U.K. Per Copy:- £18.50 - P & P - £1.45 per single copy
Multiple Copy - Subject to rebate.

Distributors:-The Archive Shop - 47-49 High Street Lydney Glos. GL15 5DD
Charles Round. P.O.Box 467 5YX Taunton. Somerset

Payment:- Cheque or Bankers Draft Make Payable To CR/Book/Fund
Credit Card:- Archive Shop - Neil & Heather Parkhouse.

Under the foregoing circumstances I can quite understand a Publisher's reluctance to become involved in such situations. Had I been aware of this at the time more cost-effective alternative would have been sought, and the trauma of the situation which developed could have been avoided.

I do not think it to be unreasonable to believe a publisher with wide promotional experience would no doubt have met a similar situations and been able to advise as to the best approach in the first instant. The publisher's actual promotional projected allocation indicated in his contract capital charges was never revealed. The actual actual amount spent in relation to allocation I believe to have been insignificant.

In the publisher's promotional strategy he fails to indicate any proposals to undertake advertisements within the media. press, magazines, technical press, radio, and television.

With capital charges below his average of £6,000 levied on an author, obviously the publisher is limited as to how he can go in that direction. I would accept not very far . However, when one is considering an author's investment of £14,000 in which a figure of £1,563 had been allocated for promotion purposes, that is quite another story.

Reflecting deeply on the situation it would seem to me better to accept a fair degree of loss on a first edition by utilising whatever monies generated there from on cost-effective advertising, rather than winding up with a heavy load of dead copies which comparatively few members of the public know about, thus giving the book little chance of resurrection.

Obviously each individual book has its own degree of uncertainty and complexity, calling for individual analysis in terms of promotional action. With a publisher's promotional experience one could expect him to be able to make a strong contribution by way of sound advice to the author. However, he could well have difficulty with such an approach – that of maintaining the morale of the author, and establishing a keen competitive edge against his more successful and more efficient contemporaries.

A further difficulty arises in that within the publishers resources - he is limited by time and financial considerations to devote much real effort to promotion without himself undertaking risk.

With the absence of merit, a book is regarded as trash and disposed to the slush pile:- an unpleasant heap of cardboard boxes, each containing a novel. It is most improbable that any single manuscript will appear as a book, or indeed come to the notice or attention of senior editors, who are highly paid and cannot waste their time dealing with such unlikely material. Research studies carried out have shown that only one in every 900 or so received ever finalises in the shape of a published book. As with many other diverse situations there is always an exception, in which a many-times rejected manuscript has blossomed into a best seller – a situation which stimulates reexamination of what is considered garbage, from time to time.

It would appear that the juniors assigned to daily work on the accumulation of rejected material cursorily glance at the contents of each manuscript retrieved. If return postage has been provided, a rejection slip is placed in the package, following which it is posted back to the sender. If there is no provision for return postage then the respective author's work is tossed into a bin, (emptied each night into huge trash containers). Experience indicates most such manuscripts to be so appaling that an examination of a single page was sufficient to warrant it's total rejection. Generally the basic shortfalls embrace mis-spelling, bizarre punctuation and badly told stories which defy any chance of success irrespective of the amount of skilled editing that could have been provided.

I can well appreciate a similar situation prevails within the United Kingdom. However, rejection irrespective of justified reason, must surely have in its wake disappointment and disillusion to whoever is involved. One has to rise above such situations, learn from mistakes, and seek to pursue whatever course is being followed with all the grit and determination one can muster, seeking advice along the way if matters become too complicated.

CAPITAL COSTS COMPARISONS - VANITY PRESS & PRINT HOUSE
My two manuscripts are considered:-
1. Machinations in Coal Mining - Vanity Press Publishers

Paperback - 236 by 156 mm - 399 pages

Capital Cost Breakdown -Typesetting	**- £4,646.00**
Printing & Binding	**- £4,048.00**
Jacket Production & Design	**- £1,234.00**
Editor	**- £1,237.00**
Promotion	**- £1,563.00**
Administrative	**- £1,730.00**
Total	**- £14,458.00**
Agreed	**- £14,000.00**

Number of Copies (Print Run) - 800

Capital Cost Per Book	**- £17.50**
Book Retail Price	**- £23.25**
Breakeven Price	**- £21.875**

Text printed single colour throughout
Two Colour cover on 270 one sided gloss (perfect bound)
Total Period of Project Execution - 12 months
4 months beyond default date.
With the absence of publishers profit the above detail to be in line with those which might be expected from a non-profit making organisation. Be that as it may - I find great difficulty in reconciling an actual "promotional expenditure of £1,563!

2. Second Manuscript
   Book Publishing Experience (A Beginners Nightmare)
   Paperback:- 216 b 156 mm. 160 pages - 4 Colour Cover
                        Capital Cost - £5,000.00
                  Number of Copies - 1,500
            Capital Cost Per Copy - £3.33
                  Breakeven Price - £4.04
                  Book Retail Price -£7.99

Total Cost includes - editing, typesetting, printing and binding, design and graphic work; and administration.

Total Period of Execution - 5 months - achieved as promised.

With the basic comparison of Per Capita Book Cost it will be noted the first manuscript cost some 5.25 times that of the second one.

PUBLISHER & PROMOTION

The book, after failing to meet two scheduled completion dates and the default date of October 31 by some eight weeks, was finally finished and published. A number of complementary copies were delivered to chosen recipients at their home addresses by December 16, 1996, ready for the Christmas holidays. This was quite a relief at the time.

However, what was to follow in terms of the book's promotion made all former difficulties, frustrations and trauma, appear to be not unlike a Sunday School outing by comparison. The publisher's concepts of what constitutes a promotional campaign differed widely from my own, in the event constituting an unbridgeable situation between the two parties, so creating difficulties on both sides.

First let us discuss the publisher's obligations under the terms of the contract:

Clause 5 (ii) - [The publisher shall be responsible for the general promotion and sales campaign of the work. He shall use his best endeavours in consultation with the author to sell as many copies as possible, and shall with the agreement of the author fix the retail price of the book. He shall also send out review copies in consultation with the author as shall be appropriate. He shall invoice and dispatch all copies sold to the trade and to individual purchasers of copies and shall account to the Author such commissions as appropriate within three months of their receipt, other than in the case of those which are sold on a "sale-or-return" basis.

Apart from the specified requirement to send out review copies, the publisher has a general promotion and sales campaign duty, with nothing more specific in connection therewith than *"He shall use his best endeavours in consultation with author to sell as many book copies as possible"* and to dispatch and account for the books that are sold.

There are no particular criteria apparent, or other means indicated by which the publisher can be judged as to what constitutes the best of his ability in such circumstances. As such it is difficult to avoid the conclusion as previously repeatedly stated a publisher's protection from his special "engineered" U.K. form of contract which has been discussed is virtually armour-plated and unassailable by the average person. Limited in means and expertise, he has little prospect of being able to mount any successful legal approach likely to give satisfaction.

Let us use "Machinations in Coal-mining" as an example and find out what really did take place concerning its promotion. At some time in or around August 1996 I received a package labelled "Promotional Strategy". This failed to make any reference to the American mail order projected solicitations involving my prepared readily-addressed list of some 350 Society of Mining Engineers members and associates, earlier discussed strategically covering the locations of the coalfields on the North American continent. Together with a similar list of U.K mining engineers and associates, this had been accepted and a verbal agreement had been taken to act on it in November 1995, the date upon which the book contract was jointly signed.

This package had apparently been rejected for the reason that it was not part of the embodiment of a promotional campaign in accordance with the contract terms.

From this situation a dispute developed, conducted by letter. It was not possible, despite initiating a meeting (considered to be unnecessary) at the publisher's production headquarters, to obtain clear intent from the publisher about his treatment of this US mail order list, on which there was failure of commitment.

Unnecessarily and unfortunately this situation developed into one of grave distrust, much wasted time and appreciable personal cost. Having spent many years during my long mining career at both the lower and highest levels of management activity, having been involved in countless contract negotiations with both workmen, trades unions, management, engineering contractors, and material and equipment suppliers, here I was finding new varieties of experience I hadn't met before.

PROMOTION STRATEGY – PUBLISHER'S APPROACH

THE promotional package for the release outlined the following people and services:

Marketing representatives – *The publisher has a team of eight marketing representatives who supply advance Information sheets and book jackets to all library suppliers and book wholesalers in the United Kingdom prior to publication. In addition they visit bookshops in the U.K. on a cyclic basis.*

Bookshops – *All the author's local bookshops are contacted. Selective specialist bookshops are contacted by direct mail with an advance information sheet, details concerning our discount terms, and ordering arrangements.*

Review copies – *It is essential that review copies are distributed, as reviews can generate considerable interest in a title. Review copies will be sent to all specialist publications and selected outlets.*

Press releases – *Press releases are sent to any newspaper which we feel might be in the author and his books best interests. Usually the newspapers are happy to feature articles concerning local authors who have their first book published. Press releases are also sent to a wide selection of specialised magazines.*

Direct mailing – *Is a highly effective form of selling books. (I found this statement difficult to reconcile, against his failure to promote the America) Mailing List formerly. It is also more financially advantageous to sell copies this way because no trade discount is applicable. Order forms and information will be sent to all organisations, societies, and individuals designated by the author, and to book clubs where appropriate upon publication.*

ADVANCE NOTICE - NEW BOOK NEWS
Single A-4 Size Notice of Book's Release.
Title. Autobiographical Sketch of Author.
New Release Notice-Book Details and Price.
BOOKSHOP CHAINS and BOOKSELLERS
BOOKSHOP CHAINS
U.K. Nationally - 25 Retailers

TAUNTON LOCALITY
1 - Bridgwater - 3 - Booksellers
2 - Wellington - 2 - Booksellers
3 - Taunton - 2 - Booksellers
4 - Minehead - 1. Bookseller.

PRESS RELEASES

LOCAL RADIO and TELEVISION
BBC Somerset Sound
BBC Radio Bristol
BBC Radio Sheffield
Radio Orchard - Taunton

TELEVISION
HTV West Taunton. Somerset
West Country Television - Plymouth Devon

LOCAL SOMERSET PRESS
1 - Burnham and Highbridge - Weekly News - Burnham on Sea
2 - Bridgwater Mercury - Bridgwater
3. Somerset County Gazette - Taunton*

4 - Somerset Magazine - Crewkerne*
5 - Star Newspapers - Tiverton
6 - Evening Post - Taunton
7 - Evening Post - Yeovil

*Responses Received

NATIONAL PRESS LONDON
1 - The Times Literary Supplement
2 - The Independent on Sunday
3 - The Mail on Sunday
4 - The Sunday Times
5 - Sunday Telegraph
6 - The Independent
7 - Sunday Express
8 - Daily Telegraph
9 - The Daily Mail
10 - Daily Express
11- The Observer
12 - The Guardian
13 - Daily Mirror
14 - The Times

*No Responses Received

REVIEW COPIES
1 - Institute of Industrial Engineering - Georgia USA
2 - Irvin Spotte - Mining Consultant - Florida, USA* (Personal)
3 - Industrial Literature Review - New York. USA
4 - Engineering News-Record - New York - USA
5 - Engineering and Mining Journal. Chicago. USA
6 - Minerals Industry International -London. UK
7 - Mining Engineering - Colorado. USA
8 - Michael Parkinson Enterprises Ltd
9 - Jack Long - President - Virginia USA* (Personal)
10 - Mining Technology, London U.K.
11- Mining Magazine, London. UK
12- Coal International - Surrey. UK
13- Mining Journal. London. UK* (Personal)
14- Pit and Quarry.

Responses Received

(Responses Received as Indicated * were the ones marked 'personal', as with some 30 or more additional ones from general readers who were private and unconnected with any society, journal, or official bodies).

Subsequently, in early summer 1997 the press and news media were approached a second time. However, no responses developed on either occasion.

In the context of the package detail as expressed, the feeling is engendered that such reviews will automatically take place, in the absence of explanation as to how such matters are dealt with and treated by the media.

Giving thought as to how the respective book review editors might decide, choose, or select the book titles for review from the countless number of books submitted to them, I can only feel their situation is not unlike that of the publisher dealing with the snowstorms of voluminous manuscripts from emerging unknown authors. Many are never properly examined, irrespective of the nature and quality of the offerings, while others are passed over with little more than a cursory glance.

Books written by celebrated and established writers, entertainers, sports personalities, public figures and politicians undoubtedly have the greatest chance of being reviewed in the press.

Perhaps review editors, not unlike the American publishing houses, have a manuscript filtering system in which books for review are so processed through the offices of sub-editors, filtered, and the surviving copies recommended as works worthy of being reviewed. The point that really matters is that in the face of what must be a heavy book review demand throughout the U.K., the book review editors can have but precious little time to judge works created by unknown authors as opposed to the voluminous range of titles produced by the many that are better known. There is the further complication that matters of current public interest, be this romantic, historic, scientific, political or adventurous, influence choice, and works with relevance to the matters of the day can be expected to rise more quickly to the top of the pile.

Book review editors, I believe, have their fingers on the nation's literary pulse and are able to stimulate that pulse from time to time. Although any form of disappointment has its emotional content, one really has to exercise personal control in this particular field of endeavour, for it is more than apparent that there are, and can be many adverse situations arising which are beyond the control of both the publisher and the author.

Under the heading Promotion Strategy reference is made to a team of eight marketing representatives supplying advance information sheets and book jackets to all library suppliers and book wholesalers in the U.K. prior to publication. In addition it says they make visits to bookshops on a cyclic basis.

Whether or not these representatives carried out their responsibilities in the direction indicated I am in no position to judge. However, leading bookstores in Teeside and Tyneside, South Yorkshire, Lancashire, Derbyshire and Nottinghamshire. were unaware of the existence of the book some two months or more after it had been released at the beginning of January 97. This apparent lapse was in addition to the failure, despite upwards of a year's lead time, to supply Whitaker's Biographical Services with the necessary detail and information with which to circulate the retail trade outlets through their respective computerised networks.

The publisher's reference to direct mailing as an effective sales system with its implied high degree of success is greatly at odds with his failure to acknowledge and implement the American list which had been accepted.

To get this in true perspective let me explain that, irrespective of who the accepted publisher was to be, I had formerly prepared two distinct mailing lists, each of some 350 ready-typed names and addresses of UK and USA Mining Engineers and Associates, in the form of guillotine-cut, paste-on transfers for the order-forms and correspondence which was to be subsequently dispatched.

How far the former UK list was adhered to I was not informed, although later circumstances dictated the need to check the situation which proved to be inconclusive.

The situation deteriorated to such an extent that legal advice was sought. As a subscriber, I approached Which? consumer group's legal department, who were very helpful, even-handed, and open-minded about the case, although concerned only with the legal aspects.

The advice given by the nominated solicitor is later reproduced with the object of providing clarification of the difficulties inherent in this situation, and with a view to giving potential help to anyone likely to be concerned in similar situations in the future.

One substantial point of interpretation relative to the contract provisions lies with the requirement firmly placed upon the publisher to *"be responsible for the general promotion and sales campaign for the work"* as opposed to his promotion strategy which, the publisher contends meets the situation. Consider the following in relation to the vital aspect of interpretation.

PROMOTION STRATEGY
BEFORE considering its format or projected activities, it is first useful to give the literary meaning ascribed to this particular heading. Collins' English Dictionary defines *Strategy* as:

> 1.the art or science of the planning and conduct of a war.
> 2.the practice or art of using stratagems, as in politics, business etc
> 3.a plan or stratagem.

And *Stratagems* as:

> 1. a plan or trick, esp. one to deceive an enemy.

One can be excused for asking the question "to whom does the noun "enemy" refer - the author, the public, or both? Irrespective of whom, what it appears to do is to legitimise under contract conditions whatever action is taken, or fails to be taken, by the publisher in relation to the contract – in which both parties are apparently engaged in hostilities.

If that is so, under the appropriate contract clause, it would appear to substantially give a high degree of flexibility to the publisher, detrimental to the 'bona fide' interests of an author or the public. **PROMOTION CAMPAIGN**

This condition refers to a campaign. It makes no reference to strategy. In this sense, something less devious and more positive is called for. Here is the dictionary definition of *Campaign*:

1. a series of coordinated activities, such as public speaking and demonstrating, designed to achieve a social, political, or <u>commercial goal; a presidential campaign, an advertising campaign</u>

No specific standards are set or definitions expressed as to the particular means apparent whereby he can be judged relative to his actions and, what is more important, no real specific activities are indicated in relation to promotional acts (refer back to, and compare once again the two alternative contracts relative to this point). No apparent period of tenure applicable to a promotional campaign, is specified. If the publisher decides to state after the book appears in print he has fulfiled all his contract obligations relative to the book's promotion, he is free to do so, with the onus of proof falling upon shoulders of the author to indicate his losses of potential sales in situations of default.

CONTRACTUAL AGREEMENT - LEGAL ASPECTS.

With further reference to the contract situation, here are the legal points of interpretation I mentioned with acknowledgments to the **WHICH?** consumer association's legal department:

1. *There is no specific list of shops in which the publisher contracts to circulate your book. Although you had various discussions with the publisher regarding circulation, the only obligation is for the publisher "to use his best endeavours to sell as many books as possible" both here and abroad.*
2. *To pursue a claim for breach of contract, a report would be required specifically confirming the losses suffered from any breach of contract by the publisher.*
3. *Confirmation as to how the steps which the publisher's failure to conform to fall short of his obligations would need to be specific. The publisher confirms various promotional activities were on the various dates. Unfortunately the information provided is not strong enough evidence of any breach, or that the activities did not take place. The only item we have in this connection is the fact (although this has not definitely been confirmed) that the publisher possibly delayed sending out the USA list until success in the UK list was ascertained. (Note: at no time, until the receipt of the information above, did the publisher indicate he was prepared to circulate the USA list, nor of any intention he had to delay its circulation).*
4. *What financial loss you have suffered, particularly in terms of lost book sales as a result of the breach, you may find difficult to quantify. You will not succeed in a claim unless you can show financial loss.*
5. *You cannot take the publisher to court just to punish them because you do not think they have promoted your book sales properly.*
6. *It is stressed the matter of financial loss cannot relate to the fact you feel*

you have made a poor commercial bargain with the publisher in terms of pricing the book. The court will generally not look into the commercial bargain that has been struck as you were free to contact with whomever you wished.

7. As well as with the specific terms set out in the agreement with the publisher, dated November 29, 1995, the law implies certain legal obligations on the part of the publisher pursuant to the Supply of Goods and Services Act of 1982. The publisher is required to perform the contract for publishing services with reasonable care and skill.

8. In such a contract, the usual remedy for breach of contract, in either the implied or specific terms of the contract, is damages to compensate the aggrieved party for what he/she has suffered. The law seeks to place that in the position he/she would have been in had the contract been performed properly.

9. The person making the claim must firstly prove a breach has taken place and then prove what financial loss has been suffered. In certain circumstances a claim may be made for inconvenience and loss of enjoyment. Awards under English Law are usually reserved for contracts whose sole purpose is for enjoyment, for instance a holiday. The person making a claim is also under legal duty to keep his or her losses to a minimum. It is stressed that you cannot under English Law obtain compensation to punish a company because you do not like the way you have been treated.

AUTHOR'S VIEWS ON PROMOTIONAL ACTIVITY

Bearing in mind the circumstances described and commented upon above I have strongly formed an opinion that the publisher has <u>no strong realistic and serious commitment in terms of promoting the books he publishes,</u> and his contract format effectively embodies a protective veneer whereby any failures relative to any commitment are both difficult to pursue, and effectively establish. I use the noun "publisher" not in its singular sense, but one within a corporate and broader sense, in which matters of the above import need to be fully addressed relative to the type of contract being considered.

In support of my views at this point, as a matter of both interest and enlightenment, here is a comment from a short article covering the Hay-on-Wye 10th Annual Festival of Literature which appeared in the New York Times on May 31 1997:

> "Because Britain lacks many of the publicity outlets that America has, most notably television talk shows with audiences of millions, and because British publishers generally spend little money on promotion, readings and personal appearances are more than ever becoming part of a writer's repertoire".

This sums up my personal situation, being far more eloquently and succinctly expressed than I feel myself capable of, and explains why amongst other things I have long been motivated by my former and current American experiences.

Hay-on-Wye is a small rural borders farming village situated on the west bank of the River Wye, which forms the boundary between Wales and the English counties of Hereford and Worcester. Although only a small village with a population of some 1,200 residents, it sustains 34 bookstores. In that year of the festival's 10th anniversary, the organisers expected that some 30,000 people would have visited by the time the last of the scheduled 160 events, featuring 250 authors in 10 days, had finished. The growing popularity of the Hay-on-Wye festivals is being considered a sign of the growing competitiveness of the literary marketplace in Britain, where authors are increasingly obliged to promote their books instead or relying on reviews and word-of-mouth to spur sales.

Having reached a virtual impasse with the publisher on the matters I had raised, my next approach was to my solicitor, **MR R.W. HEMMINGS, OF R.W.HEMMINGS AND CO., TAUNTON.** I discussed the the whole matter with him and we analysed it in great depth.

After carefully studying the mass of detail I presented his advice was simple and direct:

> *"Seek to obtain the custody of the books, having met and paid all dues involved – they belong to you – and to do whatever you wish with them".*

He then added:
> *"This will be the cleanest way, with the onus of proof being confined to having met all your financial obligations within the contract."*

Before embarking on such course, which embraced a whole new set of potential problems and difficulties, it was decided to make one further final effort to reach an acceptable agreement. This I requested the lady lawyer contacted through the Which? organisation to undertake. (By this time in addition to other matters the lawyer personified the role of a post box.). The effort was made and drew from the publisher a slight concession, to the effect he was prepared to make a "trial run" embracing a limited "mail order solicitation" selection from the contentious list of American Mining Engineers and Associates, to which careful consideration was given.

However, in an earlier letter through the Which? lawyer, attention had been drawn to an International Mining Symposium and Exhibition being held in the Doncaster (South Yorkshire) Exhibition Centre (the home of the St Leger horse race), on June 4 and 5, 1997. One of the leading exhibitors, the American Company Long Airdox Ltd, of Motherwell, Scotland, had kindly granted me facilities on their stand (one of the two largest at the exhibition) to promote my book with the help of a colleague, Mr George Smales Beedan. This was done in the hope of receiving promotional support from the publisher in a situation of limited facilities. In the event no support was forthcoming. As such there was little purpose in undertaking further negotiations.

I can do no better than reproduce relevant extracts from the letter addressed to the legal adviser, setting out the circumstances and asking her to initiate action for obtaining the custody of the books on my behalf.

"Your letter of the 6th was awaiting my return from Doncaster. This morning I received also a letter from the publisher, which I regard to be nothing more than posturing since he fails to adequately deal with my main bone of contention, which is the implementation in full of the American Mail Order Solicitation List, evaded throughout a chain of lengthy correspondence. This has long formed the basis of my basic complaint, and has given rise to the current situation. Had that been honoured in the first instance the matter would never have developed the dimensions it now has. In view of the grave omission , so far as I am concerned, I see no further point in conducting any further negotiations in the atmosphere prevailing, and in a situation in which I have no confidence.

"This new approach of trial-testing the American situation raises the question of how the united mailing list was undertaken – was that on a trial basis also? Enquiries concerning receipts of notices and proforma covered eight engineers taken at random from the U.K promotional mail order list indicated that two of the listed personnel chosen did not receive any solicitations, two were uncertain, two did, and the remaining two did not respond.

"Obviously confidence has been destroyed, at least on my side. I have formed the conclusion there is little to be gained in sustaining traumatic, bureaucratic and costly effort in the circumstances – as such I would like you to set in motion action for the recovery of all unsold copies to be collected and delivered to my address.

"This is believed to be the best course of action and avoids any requirement for the furnishing of any matter of proof on any issue by the author, other than the fulfilment of all payments scheduled against him. In the event these were all fully met prior to the book's publication.

"You will notice the publisher makes reference to the International Mining Exhibition, and his manner of treating it, as with previous occasions, as "a matter of little consequence", excusing lack of action, presumably of being ill-timely informed relative to the event. The publisher would appear to have had sufficient time to initiate some supportive action. Maybe you could kindly check your dates of your correspondence to him relative to this matter.

"The twenty outstanding books he formerly promised in previous correspondence would have been immensely useful, and could readily have been sold as signed copies, but again I was inadequately supported. However I did actually let one lady have my only copy (the one you returned to me). I could not refuse her entreaties.

"The visit to the International Mining Exhibition in Doncaster was a great success in many ways (within the limited facilities available). Some 30 to 40 people were interviewed re the book – it being widely considered to be a fine book worthy of the widest possible exposure in libraries, historic institutions,. societies and working class homes as a work of heritage importance."

"Our efforts were on the proverbial shoe-string, two copies (my one remaining copy and that of my Scottish engineering friend) being the only exhibits available. Long Airdox Ltd produced for me an A4 sized framed book cover for display purposes favourably and conveniently placed and projected to command the notice of visitors to the stand.

"Criticism came from a number of Selby coalfield miners, in that the book at £23.25 retail and £25.25 mail order was priced too high for them despite its family appeal and suitability for heritage retention. The same point was made by pensioners , redundant miners, and others.

"Through my nephew's wife Dorothy Round's initiative I was able to enjoy a fabulous 30-minute over the air radio chat with Tony Capstick, a very popular Radio Sheffield and South Yorkshire presenter (covering a catchment area of some 2,000.000 people), during which a phone call established contact with the son of former colliery official and supporting colleague. He recalled as a boy meeting me during breakfast at his home. on one occasion.

"Tony Capstick really had read and understood the book in great depth, and commented most enthusiastically of its value as a document worthy of a strong and wider public exposure. He himself found it to be particularly informative, valuable and an enjoyable book to read. (an audio tape copy was kindly produced for me).

"Further to the foregoing I have managed to get the National Caphouse Exhibition Mine (formerly an operating mine under my control), Wakefield, West Yorkshire, interested in the sale of the book subject to acceptable discounts.

"This situation further serves to show what I have repeatedly tried to get across – the publisher's commitment to effect real promotion had no meaningful substance.

"In the circumstances outlined, I merely propose to acknowledge the publisher's letter (copy attached), indicating that I have instructed you as to the action I would like you to take."

However, as formerly stated, no real progress was being made in that the legal adviser's remit did not allow joint-working alongside one's private solicitor. She withdrew her services. at this point.

Despite the final breakdown of relationships, her contribution was both useful and helpful. I have no doubts in my mind that, but for taking this step of initiating legal action, no progress would have been made.

It was really the failure to provide the promotional support we required to augment our efforts at the Doncaster International Mining Exhibition and Convention, and the off-handed way with which this lack of support was dismissed, that tipped the scales and prompted me to instruct my solicitor to serve notice for the unsold book copies *to be delivered into the author's custody at his private address and to be used there at in whatever manner he decides.*

The instruction was carried out and the publisher dispatched 20 large boxes (total 640 copies) of the remaining stock, these being received on July 9, 1997,.at my home address. As anticipated, receipt of the books gave rise to a new set of problems. All connection with the retail and mail order outlets had been severed, while housing all the books in my small external working office had it virtually bursting at the seams.

On August 5, 1997, I received a book balance sheet which as stated, as had earlier been indicated, that a shortfall of 62 books was un-accounted for, with no explanations given. At £17.5 a copy this equates to £1,085.

COMPLIMENTARY COPIES

A complimentary copy is sent to each individual nominated by the author together with a compliments slip. In all 28 official complimentary copies were dispatched in accordance with the above, mainly to family members and close friends.

A further 32 promotional copies were distributed, 12 to the United States and 20 within the United Kingdom by myself.

A new set of communications had now to be established, incorporating an approach to the potential American market.

In hindsight, and taking into account subsequent experiences, it seems that but little merit can be credited to either the publisher or myself. in allowing the situation to develop as it did into an entrenched and inflexible battle of attrition. As an example of how to resolve common problems it was a public relations disaster.

Had I been a consultant or adviser one of my main recommendations would have been for the publisher to give consideration to the employment of an experienced and skilled public relations officer with direct responsibilities to himself, which would free both his departmental heads and himself from dealing with irksome and time consuming difficulties, in whatever form they take, in order to concentrate on increasing organisational efficiency in line with the best examples of fair trading practice. Such a person could put meaningful content within the company policy as set in the executive editor's letter dated October 18, 1995, (at least insofar as my experience is concerned). Moreover, lapses within the publisher's organisation and shortfalls in performance highlighted by the authors so affected could be more effectively identified, investigated, corrected and – equally importantly – properly explained, as opposed to a dismissive overbearing approach, or rising to the defence of ones staff irrespective of the circumstances (a situation which is neither helpful to the individual or the organisation he or she serves). Criticism and complaint may be irksome and disrupting, but they do have importance as indicators, identifying the need for change and revision in undetected deteriorating situations and shortfalls in performance.

Treating authors as children, or as illogical or stupid persons, is certainly not an endearing or constructive way to enhance public relations, or to get the best co-operative results to the joint satisfaction of all parties, particularly the public in the last analysis.

In traumatic periods of event when one feels to be in a state of uncontrollable descent a point of "rock bottom" is often reached in which a feeling of things "can get no worse" seems to be the situation:-

"but they do"

We lost "Kim" our family pet in December 1997.

TITLE'S ACCEPTANCE BY THE PUBLIC

WHATEVER one's feelings are concerning the public's apparent lack of interest in or demand for his or her product, and the capital losses associated with this, to receive letters of praise from readers is a satisfying compensation. This is particularly true of those received from senior citizens free from inhibitions, and obviously happy with their nostalgic recollections, induced by some matter or other which has caught their attention within the book they have picked up and read, irrespective of the author's lack of reputation.

In my case, over a period of some 12 months upwards of 30 or more readers have taken the trouble to relay to me their impressions. Here are some examples:

From Mr. Albert Williams, retired miner, March 1, 1997 –
Having been introduced to your book by an old friend, George Beedan, I was told of my Uncle Harry being mentioned. I was very interested. My son bought me the book for a birthday present. I am not an avid reader but I started to read the book and I couldn't put it down.

It was of the greatest interest reading about my wife's grandparents and the family of Emmett Walker. My wife's father was Robert Emmett Walker (oldest son).

The Walker name has now ceased (brother-in-law – no family; Jim's son – no family). I recall being trained by a young Mr C. Round. I was 18 years old. I vividly remember Tommy Farmer training with us. Tommy was about 32 years old. It seemed strange as we all thought Tommy was an old man. He was the former projectionist at the cinema . The training level was at the back of the stables. I recall on the first day on that level I saw old Clarrie Bott having his snap in a manhole. It really scared me.

Referring to the ventilation work, my pal Maurice Short and I were your assistants. We started Saturday morning at the downcast, travelling to the South Level Thorncliffe Drift return paddy road. It was nearly midnight when we got to the fan shaft bottom. I recollect the paddy train was some distance from the pit bottom and had broken down. Glad it was Mr Round who had to do the calculations. What I like about the book is your honesty. Uncle Harry used to tell us what a hard job you had. He said the telephones never stopped ringing when you got home. By the way, my birthday isn't while April and I have read the book – my son let me have it early. so you know how much I enjoyed it.

My wife and I were talking to the Lord Mayor and I told him about the book. His reply was "we've already got it". I will close now hoping my letter is readable as I am not a great letter writer. Hope you are well. Remember me to Dorothy and family. I knew Dorothy but not your son John. Thanks once again for the pleasure of reading your book.

Albert Williams.

P.S. I remember Maurice Beedan nearly taking our chimney pots off in the plane.

The work Mr Williams refers to was a special job connected with the ventilation of new coal seam workings at Earl Fitzwilliam's (Wentworth) Elsecar Main Colliery, Barnsley, South Yorkshire, which was being developed at the time and dates back over 50 years. The following is the most recent letter received - from a Lady - 31.01.1998

From Mrs Kathleen Burkinshaw, Littlemoor, Ashover, Derbyshire –

Let me introduce myself – my name is Kathleen Burkinshaw, my father was James W. Nixon, a winding engineman, and my father-in-law was Cecil Burkinshaw, a deputy. Both worked at Wharncliffe Silkstone Colliery through my childhood there, and I consider myself fortunate to have lived in the village and to have been part of that community.

My daughter now has young children for whom I am attempting to write about my early life. Naturally the village and the pit are my base line.

I recently bought your book, Machinations In Coal-mining, and have enjoyed reading your story, especially your early days living in Hoyland Common and starting work at Wharncliffe Silkstone Colliery. I greatly admire your determination to succeed.

I don't aspire to writing for publication, just details for my family and their children. My stories would be mainly about social aspects and growing up in a pit village. At the same time I would like the facts to be relevant and to show their place in local history. I remember a lot about the pit, but there is still such a lot that I have forgotten. I wonder if you would be good enough to test your memory for me. I have done quite a lot of research, and have collected a good, selection of books, photographs and newspaper cuttings.

When my father first worked as a winder he worked three shifts, days afternoons and nights. To change from days to afternoons he had to work a twelve hour shift. This happened on a Sunday and I had to take his Sunday dinner to him in the winding house. I would often stay a few hours fascinated by this steam winding engine (No.

4). He would take me to see the No. 1 engine and we would explore every corner of Wharncliffe Silkstone and he would explain every aspect of coal mining to me.

We visited the boiler house where your father worked and I remember the boilerman would open the firedoors to show me inside, and tell me that people brought their dead dogs and cats to be burned. Was it true? I don't know. I also enjoyed visiting the blacksmith's shop where my uncle, Albert Nixon, worked.

Thank you for reading my letter and if you think you could help me to remember I would be pleased.

Kathleen Burkinshaw.

As a winding engineman in those days Mrs Burkinshaw's father carried very heavy responsibilities in the raising and lowering of men from and into the mine workings at a depth of 654 feet. During the winding of men operations upwards of 80 men could be travelling up and down the mine shaft at any one time – that is 40 going into the mine and 40 coming out. Overwinding was always a fear in such situations - if and when they occurred the result was a serious disaster with terrible injuries being sustained by the miners involved. Winding enginemen were special people apart – usually men of high rectitude.

My final choice is from the seasoned and successful author and playwright Barry Hines, a miner's son born within my own village, Hoyland Common. His book **"KES"** received great acclaim and was produced as a very successful film bearing the same title.

From Mr Barry Hines, Sheffield, South Yorkshire –

I think it is an excellent book combining technical expertise with good stories. I think it is a mining classic.

Quite a number of readers telephoned their observations and comments – it really is good to have a personal chat with someone who not only expresses his/her opinions but often gives the background to their personal situation.

My failure to adequately undertake research into the book publishing business prior to starting my adventures in authorship is to some extent can be excused by having produced a "quality work" as suggested by the following comment, which appeared in the *"Archive"* March Issue (No.17. 1998) of the Quarterly Journal for British Industrial and Transport History published by the Lightmoor Press of Lydney, Gloucestershire.

The reviewer is Tony Oldham.

This is a fascinating autobiography of a man who left secondary school without any qualifications and started work at the age of 14 as an underground pony driver. By sheer hard work at night school and technical college, he qualified at an early age as a mining engineer. He soon progressed through general management posts to the highest area production and planning managerial positions.

This book will appeal to a wide audience, both technical and non-technical, and will take its place as an invaluable and essential historical record of the British mining industry from the pick and shovel, steam engine, belt driven era, to the modern, fully powered, coal-cutting, road-driving, roof-supporting, underground coal and personal transport system age, with its vastly improved productivity and safety.

The author is a brilliant engineer and, throughout the book, one is impressed by his ingenuity in designing and re-designing coal-mining equipment. The constant drive to achieve a fully mechanised scenario increased production by over twenty times. Unfortunately, this came too late to save the industry from the savage effects of the Thatcher Government.

The author is also a dazzling diplomat well able to negotiate with top management or at shop floor level. The difficulties in overcoming backward looking practices – management by fear and small minds in big jobs – are vividly portrayed. In every position he held bar one, he was able to increase productivity.

He describes many well known personalities and was on first name terms with Lord Robens. Some Coal Board members proved to be difficult people to get on with and his warts-and-all vignettes of these folk will provide lawyers with work for many years to come.

Finally, management within the NCB proved too much and he took early retirement at the age of 58. Following this, he undertook mining consultancy work for a number of years, with assignments emanating the UK to Spain and the USA

In the same journal, Neil Parkhouse comments as follows –

He now has possession of the remaining unsold copies and the Archive Shop has agreed to act as distributor on his behalf. The shame is, as Tony Oldham's review indicates, that this is actually an excellent and important piece of work, which most industrial publishers would have been happy to take on, and is deserving of a far wider audience. Charles has accepted that the trade price of the book will leave him with a substantial loss. but it is his desire that this account of his life's work is made available to mining historians as readily as possible. He has, however, bounced back from this setback in fine style. His latest book is a testimony in dealing with the sort of pitfalls as he encountered in the Machinations and how to avoid them – Not bad for a man of 84!

SALES PROGRESS

THE period covered lies between December 16, 1996, and February 28, and is covered in three parts:

1. Publisher's activities December 16, 1996-July 6, '97 Original Print Run 800 copies specified in contract.

Publisher's written statement stock allocation and disposals, July 1997: Stock Allocation for "Machinations in Coal Mining"

Opening Stock **738**
File Copy.......................................**1**
Copyright Copies **6**
To Durham Office...........................**24**
Damaged Copy..................................**1**
Copies Dispatched To Author **634**
Copies Dispatched as Orders **72**
Indirect Sales - 38 Copies **52.78%**
Direct Sales - 34 ....**47.22%**
Grand Total Accounted For:-73 copies

Hereto I have referred to a "Compensating Factor" in relation to "direct Sales percentages" in connection with easily calculating the values of "breakeven prices, sales and profits with 50 per cent direct sales and 40 per cent discounted sales this works out at 0.80. On the actual percentages quoted above the Compensating Factor works out at 0.81 – where applied to the Computer Spreadsheet this value is automatically developed.

2. Author's Activities, period July 8, 1997-March31, 1998. Promotional Activities - Local press, colleges, historical and working men's institutions in South Yorkshire were all solicited as potential sales avenues. Serious and determined efforts in terms of media advertising undertaken.

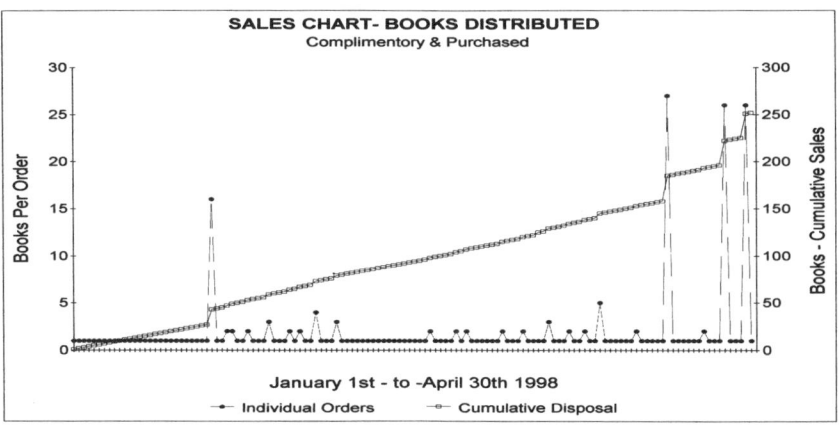

SALES CHART- BOOKS DISTRIBUTED
Complimentory & Purchased

January 1st - to -April 30th 1998
—•— Individual Orders   —□— Cumulative Disposal

SOURCE COST

COAL AGE - USA Mining Magazine £440.00
(Vol. 102 - No.12 Dec: 1997)

ADMAG UK - Tyne and Teeside Coverage £250.00
(Four Issues - Weekly - Dec: 97)

ADMAG UK - South Yorks and Nottinghamshire £122.00
(One Issue Sheffield and Nottingham - Dec 97)

MAIL ORDER SOLICITATIONS...£300.00
(Librarians - South Yorks, Notts and Derbys, Durham and Northumberland.)

Total Cost of Advertisements:-£1,116.00

Despite the author having taken over his book stock, the publisher's sales and distribution staff kindly forwarded all subsequent orders they received through to myself for processing. Eight such copies were involved.

The sales chart above shows the sales situation in full – inclusive of review complimentary, and promotional copies, together with the actual sales revenues and discounts.

Total Book Disposals – Publisher and Author = 213 copies:-

Revenue Accrued – £2,703.

Over the Period Dec '97 to March '98 inclusive –

Total Disposals to March 31 = 213

Total Revenue Received was = £2,703

Total Losses After 15 months' trading = ((£14,000+ £1116) - £2,702 }

= £15,116 - £2702 = £12,414

To make up the cost of the advertisements, £1,116.00, 80 books needed to have been sold.
10 books were sold in total in response to advertising effort.

REMAINDERS
REFERENCE has already been made to unsold or remaindered copies. After as

short a period as 12 months, if a book moves slowly and the commercial publisher finds himself embarrassed by the heavy cost of stock being serviced, it can be remaindered. In such cases the stock is sold off at a nominal value and finds its way into avenues other than normal booksellers. It is also heavily discounted, such that popular works by highly credited and popular authors are often sold for fractions of their initial launching retail price. In vanity and subsidised press situations it can take two or three or more years before this happens, or any length of time specified in a contract. A trip round some superstores and large book stores will generally confirm that situation. To me, this should be an important factor to be considered in the fixing of the elemental factors in the initial contract. With the fixing of a high book price, as I have said earlier, the competitive edge is blunted. High book prices do not necessarily mean high profit, particularly when they put off buyers.

FINAL COMMENT & OBSERVATIONS

Throughout the book I have tried to be constructive and factual, solely with the object of providing "feedback" to the publishing trade, and help to "first edition authors" in identifying and circumventing the sort of problems and difficulties encountered in the writing and the Vanity Press publishing of my first book, Machinations in Coal Mining, considered by high authorities as an excellent, historic and valuable account of the "coal mining industry" over the past 75 years.

Moreover I have also tried to consider the genuine publisher's situation, as I feel the unscrupulous ones to be in a minority.

The natural difficulties which beset an "unknown–first time writer" attempting to gain public acclaim and recognition, are indeed formidable. As such the genuine publisher, agent, packager, and others have much to offer such gifted and other like personages in the evolution of their manuscript as "published books".

The sort of experiences outlined, although irksome and traumatic I do not consider to have been abortive. They have a useful part to play in the scheme of things, if they are analysed and the lessons learned are later applied. The fact of having disposed of some 400 copies involving a substantial loss of some £8,000 to £10,000 is truly disconcerting, but there are other gains which cannot be evaluated in monetary terms.

Sadly "The nation is not remotely interested in the mining industry. If there is a pit disaster, they are heroes–if there is a wage claim they are militants but as to the rest they simply do not want to know"–*(quotation, page 338–The Benn Diaries, 1995)*

This situation still obtains, motivating my desire to ensure that the coal mining industry will not be forgotten for its great economic contribution over the years, to the welfare of each and every one of us in one form or another.

I have no doubt my ideas are open to controversy–I hope so–such that something better will emerge to give the unknown "first edition author" a better chance than he/she currently has–(the Nations corporate intellect and imagination needs to be developed on a scale vastly surpassing anything that has gone before).

Whilst there are moves taking place to curb the excesses of those nefarious "vanity press" publishers through attempted legislation there is much we members of the public accomplish in checking those excesses. As such I hope I have been able to indicate how this may be done, particularly in terms of price fixing stressed repeatedly throughout the narrative.

The "profitability sketches" relative to my two manuscripts show a serious "first edition writers anomaly" in which the current practice of "retailers discount" on the books he processes–whatever the cause:-

"penalises a writer and rewards a retailer, the more costly a book is taken to produce" at the former's and indeed indirectly the public's expense"

BOOK RETAIL OUTLETS

Much has been said relative to a "books promotion" in terms of a Publisher. Let us now examine the situation relative to the publishing trades "National Book Retail Outlets" and the support and encouragement as a "first time author" one receives from such outlets. Virtually "nil"! An approach to the higher levels in relation to getting a book in the windows or on the shelves – purchased or otherwise, met with a response "such matters are vested in the Retail Stores Local Management" – reference back to such Management autonomy – invariably met with the "need of approval from Headquarters." Maybe this in entrenched bureaucracy – whatever, it is dispiriting to the "first time author".

Let the "first edition" author seek to find his book or reference to it, in a store following its release. He or she had better be prepared for an abortive experience, in so far as his/her interests are concerned.

The small "bookstore" has problems. Discussions with one such Bookshop Proprietor in Barnsley (with its long tradition in Coal Mining). South Yorkshire, was quite illuminating. Look at the book offered "with its high degree of excellence" prompted the observation – I could sell this, but it would need to be much less than the £23.25 imprinted on the paperback cover – no more than half the price. You are going to have trouble." Another Proprietor stated "I can't afford to invest such amounts in a book nobody is aware of in the absence of former or current publicity." A third Proprietor – looked at the Publisher's name and immediately turned to me and said: "Are these people serious?", and again commented on the book price – as a deterrent.

Early royalties indicated discounts of £10.25 on the book's retail price of £23.25 had been made to the Big Boys, i.e. – 44.08%. This aspect of the trade – I have not been able to research for obvious reasons but nevertheless, it has been subjected to much thought and application – particularly as discounts are on the basis of the Retail Book Price. Examining the potential rewards to the Bookseller in relation to the risk-factor it would appear a wide range of facets exist in which a bookseller could:-

1. Purchase a "test run" strategically stocked and placed in his organisation to best effect – his total highest risk factor.

2. Accept copy on a "sale or return" basis – in which his risks are confined to servicing cost reduction total risk.

3. Operate on the basis of "Processing Orders" referred to him, a minimal or no risk situation.

Since he receives a first edition fixed discount on the books which flow through his organisation irrespective of how: the third approach would seem the most rewarding, particularly where such orders have been generated by sources external to his organisation. However to me I see a serious anomaly respect to the authors interests. Presumably the Bookstore operates a "standard system" (computer network as an example) with each order he receives being processed in a like manner. Whilst no two books may be alike – each processed order presumably is handled in a like manner. Yet on the basis of discounted sales the rewards in terms of fixed percentages (44% quote as an example). The higher a book costs to produce – the greater the reward to the retailer – irrespective of what the publisher has taken. This is shown in the Chart A Writer's Anomaly.

Summarising the details show on the Chart for the two books I have written taking a 40 per cent sales discount and 50 per cent sales split we have:

ELEMENT Per Copy	PUBLISHERS EFFORT Book I	AUTHORS EFFORT Book II
Capital	£14,**000**	**£5,000**
Print Run	800	1,500
Pre Capita Price	£17.50	£3.33
Breakeven	**£21.87**	**£4.16**
Retail Book Price	**£23.25**	**£7.99**
Apparent Profit	£1.37	£3.82
Retailer Profits	£9.30	£3.196
Authors Profits	£7.93 Loss/Copy	**£0.63**

The profit the publisher takes from the servicing of the first manuscript is as formerly stated indeterminable – although it would not in this case be any surprise to me were I later to discover it to be well over £5.00 per copy.

Finally I would suggest to readers, not to be discouraged by what has been written–but at the same-time not to be emotionally carried away with what appears to be Vanity Press accolades, promises and publicity hype.

ACKNOWLEDGEMENTS

I express my thanks and appreciation to the "Which?–Consumer's Legal Service" for their generous help and advice.

To Mr R.W. Hemmings of "R. W. Hemmings & Co" Solicitors, Taunton, Somerset for his help, advice and encouragement in checking "proofs" with

DISCOUNTS BASED ON RETAIL PRICES
A WRITER'S ANOMALY

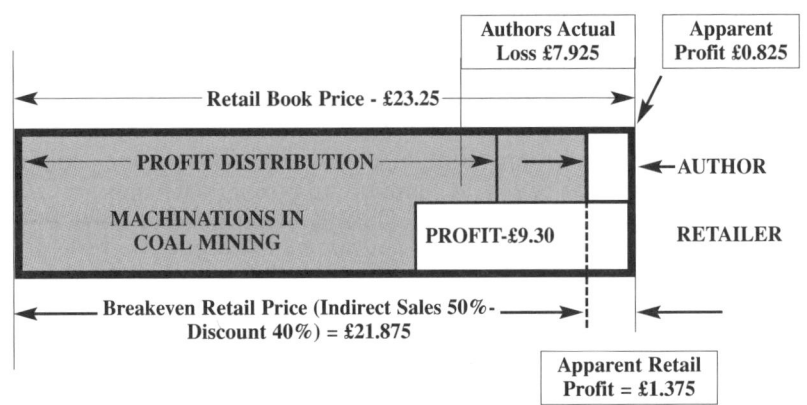

MANUSCRIPT – NO. 1

EXAMPLE NO. 1

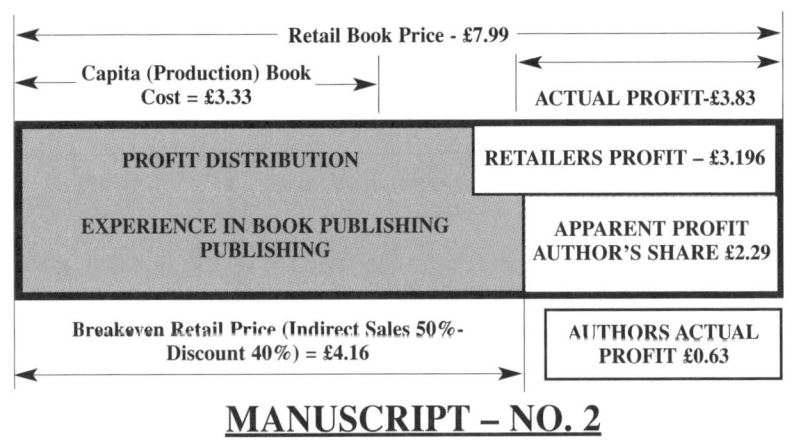

MANUSCRIPT – NO. 2

EXAMPLE NO. 2

Shaded Area's Authors Costs of Production

both manuscripts–I offer my sincere thanks and appreciation.

For permission to use the extracts from "The Tony Benn Diaries" I express my thanks and appreciation–to Mr Tony Benn MP, Westminster Palace.

To Neil and Heather Parkhouse "The Archive Shop", 47-49 High Street, Lydney, Gloucestershire–I extend my thanks and appreciation for all the help and support they have so generously provided.

I express my gratitude to "Mr Adrian Haines" of "Artytype", 5 The Marina, Harbour Road, Lydney, Gloucestershire, for his help and that of his Company in producing this book, a contrastingly pleasurable experience as compared with former efforts.

My grateful thanks I append to my niece by marriage, Mrs Dorothy Round–her kindness has been and continues to be overwhelming.

I express with great pleasure my thanks and appreciation to Derek Irwin a local neighbour for his kind interest, encouragement, unstinted friendship and practical support throughout.

Finally it would be most remiss were I not to refer to my friend and colleague George Smales Beedam of Wainwright Avenue, Wombwell, Barnsley, South Yorkshire–whose help and support has sustained me through a number of setbacks and disappointments. He has my enduring and grateful thanks.

Charles Round

APPENDIX: A BRIEF SUMMARY OF AMERICAN PUBLISHING TERMS

A.A: Author's alterations – Changes made by the author during proof reading.

Acid-free paper: Paper which is free from acids or other destructive ingredients, for archival and historic works, family histories, libraries and non-circulating or low-circulating editions.

Advance copies: Copies of a book dispatched to customers immediately it rolls the press, before the rest of the print run is shipped.

Alignment: The positioning of print on a page in alignment with that on an adjacent page and the reverse side of the same page.

Air/White Space: Additional space, between lines, margins, or artwork to circumvent the appearance of a page looking crowded or unduly dark.

Appendix: Material placed at the back of a book. Although related to the text, it is not essential.

Art/Artwork: Sketches, plans, drawings, photographs, illustrations and paintings.

Author-Publisher: A self publishing author who has applied for ISBNs and has set up the publishing himself or through the services of a packager.

Back Lining: A strip of paper of fabric used to strengthen the spine of a casebound book.

Back flap: The back inside fold of a dust jacket – usually providing a photograph and biographical detail of the author together with the author's imprint.

Black Matter: The selections at the end of a book embracing appendix glossary, bibliography, index, and related material.

Bad Break: Starting a page or ending with a widow, or orphan, or other messy looks, inappropriate hyphenation in a word at the end of a line.

Bar Code: A series of electronically decipherable vertical bars encoded with the title, ISBN and book price.

Binder Board: A stiff high-grade composition board used in book-binding. The cloth is glued over it to make the case or hard cover.

Bleed: An image or colour that extends beyond the trim edge of the page, or from one page to another in a spread.

Bluelines (blues):   Bluelines, like architectural drawings, are photoprints made from stripped negatives or positives, used to check the position of the elements and assuring the pages are in order. Not to be used for final proofing. Bluelines must be approved and returned quickly to keep book production on schedule.

Body copy: The primary or main part of the text.

Body text: Type used for body copy – it may be different from that

	used for headings.
Boldface:	Heavier face type to make the words stand out.
Book block:	The sewn and trimmed signatures which are ready bound, with everything put together but the cover.
Book cloth:	The special cloth used for book covers. In a similar manner to linens, the quality is determined by the number of threads per inch and their strength.
Book manufacturing:	The specialised process of printing and binding the book.
Book packaging:	A process by which a self-publishing author contracts to have his book produced by a professional agent, one in which he receives the entire press run.
Book style:	Adherence to an accepted set of standard abbreviations, spellings and punctuation.
Bound galley:	A copy of the finished book, uncorrected page proofs, or manuscripts, bound with a cheap cover, and sent to reviewers who want to see the book in advance of publication. Sometimes called "cranes" after the company that originally produced them.
Browser:	A software package such as Netscape or Microsoft Explorer that guides the user through the World Wide Web and displays HTML codes as text and graphics.
Bulk:	The thickness of a book without the cover. Heavier papers can "bulk" up a book to make it thicker, important in situations in which "thin volumes" must have a certain thickness where they are to be casebound.
C.1.S.:	Coated one side. Papers used for paperback covers and dust jackets have an enamel coating on one side.
C.2.S.:	Coated two sides. Both sides of the paper enamelled – used for paperbacks.
Camera ready:	The material is ready for reproduction – the final copy is ready.
Case bound:	Another term for "hard cover".
Cataloguing in Publication/CIP:	Information for catalogue card provided by the American Library of Congress. (after its review of the manuscript) or by some distributors for inclusion on the copyright page.
Coated paper:	Mineral and chemical substances referred to as enamel, that are applied to the paper to produce greater opacity or brightness, with glossy or matt finish.
Coffee-table book:	Large book with many Ilustrations, often with coloured photographs, or prints for the purpose of display.
Colour key:	An overlay proof composed of individual coloured acetate sheets for each of the PMS colours used by the printer, used

	to check register, obvious blemishes and size.
Colour Proof:	A laser proof showing the approximate colours of the cover or artwork, used to check register for errors.
Copyright:	Ownership of the work, protected by law. Copyright should be in the name of the owner – the author, publisher, or whoever paid for the work.
Corner marks:	Open parts of squares placed on original copy as a position guide. Shows the actual size of the book pages – sometimes known as crop or printer's marks.
Crop/Crop marks:	To crop is to eliminate a part of a photograph or other illustration. Crop marks show the area to be saved, or to be eliminated.
Customer's service rep, C.S.R:	The service representatives at the book manufacturer who is assigned to each project. Good representatives will shepherd a book through the printing and binding process facilitating production and other schedules.
DPI:	Dots per inch. The more dpi, the sharper the reproduction. Books should be printed at no less and preferably more than 600 dpi for good quality reproduction – most lasers output at only 300 dpi.
Distributor:	The middle man between the publisher and the retail outlet.
Drop ship:	To ship an order to one address and bill charges to another.
Duotone:	A two-colour halftone reproduction from a monotone original.
Dust jacket:	The printed paper cover or book jacket wrapped around a casebound book.
E-mail:	Correspondence, mail or messages etc, dispatched electronically, using an Internet connection through an Internet server (American-On-Line [AOL], Microsoft Network, etc). The server link needs to be established before links with others can be created.
Editor:	A person who prepares a manuscript for publication, one who can help breathe life into a manuscript, and assist with style and check for accuracy.
EM dash or space:	EM – a unit of measure in typesetting equal to point size of the type in question. An em dash is always used instead of a double hyphen to indicate a change of thought in a sentence.
EN dash or space:	Half the size of an em. An en-dash is used instead of an hyphen to interspace a range of dates or numbers.

Endsheets:	Two pages of strong paper wrapped round a book block of a casebound book, with one leaf of each pasted to the `inside board of the case. Can be plain or printed with colours or designs.
Extract:	Section of material taken from another book, set in smaller type or indented.
Fax:	An inexpensive and speedy electronic means to send printed or written information, receive orders and communications via telephone circuits.
F and G:	Folded and gathered but not yet bound into a book block.
Facing pages:	Two pages that face each other when the book is open.
Film lamination:	A process of bonding plastic film to the cover to protect it from scratching and improve appearance.
Font:	Full assortment (upper and lower case, numerals, symbols, etc in various sizes) of a specific style of type.
Foreword:	A statement by an expert (not the author) in the front matter, not to be confused with 'forward', which means to advance or move ahead.
Front flap:	Usually features as a synopsis or teaser about content, the price and ISBN.
Front matter:	The front section (foreword, preface, introduction, etc) with pages numbered in Roman numerals that come before the book body.
Fulfilment house:	A place where orders, usually for single copies, are taken and books shipped. Will have credit card capability and will take 800 calls in 24 hours.
Galley/galley proof:	Typeset material before it has been formatted into book form.
Gutter:	The blank space between columns of type or text and spine.
Gray scale:	A scale of gradations of grey to black. It measures the range and contrast of scanned images.
Half-title page:	The page in the front matter containing only the book title. or section title. It precedes the title page and is often used as the autographing page.
Hard copy:	The paper printout of what is on your computer screen.
Halftone:	A photographic image that has been printed through a screen composed of minute dots. This breaks up the image so that it can be reproduced with proper contrast in the printing process.
Header:	The headline at the beginning of a chapter (chapter head) or the beginning of a section (section head) or a new topic (subhead).
High Contrast:	The darkness between adjoining areas is well defined,

	sometimes greater than in the original photograph.
Home page:	The index or menu page of a Web site. The page that the user will be taken to first, and from which they can go to all parts of the Web site.
HTML:	Hypertext Modifying Language – the coding language used to mark up Web sites.
Imprint:	The identifying name of the publishing company which printed the book,
Independent publisher:	A publishing house which is not publicly owned or one of the "Big Guys".
International Standard Book Number (ISBN):	A number assigned to the publisher that identifies each book. The ISBN should be printed on the copyright page, the back cover and the spine.
Internet:	A system of worldwide communication over telephone lines and satellite links which is available through Internet providers (usually local).
ISBN:	See International Standard Book Number.
Italic:	Sloped letters. If needed for emphasis, use sparingly! Also used to mark titles of book and magazines in text.
Justify:	To have the text set flush left and/or right. The lines of text are squared off and type is spaced to evenly fill the line. Most books are justified.
Kerning:	Adjusting the space between two characters for aesthetics so they appear closer together or further apart.
Layout:	A working diagram of how the page(s) will look for an artist, typesetter or printer to follow as a guide.
Leaders:	Rows of dots or dashes to guide the eye across a page. Use sparingly. Try to avoid using them in the table of contents.
Leading:	The space between each line of type, measured from baseline to baseline and expressed in points.
Leaf:	Each piece of paper in the book, with a page on each side.
Library binding:	A stronger heavily reinforced binding that meets the standards of the American Library Association.
Link(s):	Hyperlinks – coded and highlighted words or icons in an HTML document that, when clicked, will transport a Web user to another page in a Web site or even to another site in the Web.
Long run:	A print run of 10,000+ copies.
Marketing:	Finding out what the pubic wants and meeting its needs. A self-publishing author's responsibility.
Mass market paperbacks:	Books produced inexpensively for distribution in

	supermarkets, drug stores, and some bookstores. Usually small, approximately 4.5 by 6 inches, and produced in quantity at low cost.
Match print:	A photographic print of four-colour cover of page made from the film that the plates will be made from. Used by the pressman to check accuracy of colour as they are printed.
Matt:	Dull finish. No lustre or gloss.
Mechanicals:	Copy that uses overlays to indicate the position and register of each element or colour to be printed. Colour key.
Moisture content:	A measure of relative humidity that expresses the amount of water in the paper.
NAIP:	National Association of Independent Publishers.
NAIPR:	National Association of Independent Publishers' Representatives.
Nocurl paper:	A new process that keeps paper covers from curling up in high humidity.
Offset lithography:	A printing process in which image area and non-image area exists on the same plate and are separated by chemical repulsion.
Orphan:	The first line of a paragraph that is left at the bottom of a page. Orphans signal lack of professionalism in book formatting.
Otabind	One of several patented binding processes that adapt perfect binding so that the book can lie flat without being held open.
Out of register:	Pages on both sides of a sheet or colours that are not aligned.
Printer's error (PE):	A necessary correction or change caused by an error by the printer or typesetter that is not billed to the customer.
PPI (pages per inch):	The number of pages contained in one inch stack of paper. Varies depending upon the weight of the paper.
Page:	One side of a leaf.
Page proof:	Proof of type in page form. The final proofs before going to camera copy.
Paperbound:	Paperback or softcover book.
Perfect bound:	A binding method which uses flexible adhesive to hold each page in place after folds along the spine have been cut off. Most paperback books are perfect bound.
Pick'n pack:	A shipping house that will store and ship books. Orders are faxed to them, following which they pick, pack and ship books to the required destination on behalf of the initiator.

	Some also have fulfilment services.
Plastic comb binding:	Also called spiral or GBC binding. A type of binding made of rolled rigid plastic cut in the shape of a comb or rake, and inserted through slots punched in the spine edge of book pages. Cookbooks and workbooks are often bound this way..
Preface:	Part of front matter.
Prelims:	Preliminary pages or front matter.
Prepress:	All manufacturing setup work prior to going on the press.
Process colours:	yellow, cyan, blue, magenta, red and black. Thousands of colours can be produced using these colours in various combinations.
Publisher:	The company or person whose IBSN is applied to the book, whose imprint appears on the title page and who presents the literary product to the public.
Publisher's rep:	A person who tries to sell books to a distributor, wholesaler, or to independent stores.
Questions about book packaging:	Call Tabby House for free consultation during business hours (EST) (942) 628-9-7646, or e-mail Publisher@Tabby House.
Ragged right:	Type that is justified on the left margin and is unjustified on the right.
Resolution:	The degree of sharpness in either screen display or an image, measured in dots per inch. A low resolution (72dpi) is used in newspaper printing and for computer screen images, while higher resolutions (300 or 600 dpi) are used in laser printers.. Higher resolution (1200 to 2450 dpi) comes from laser printers and image setters.
Retail:	Selling to the general public at the stated price of the product.
Recto:	A right hand odd-numbered page.
Roman type:	a regular typeface, as opposed to italic or boldface versions of the type.
Rules:	Vertical or horizontal lines on a page.
Run:	Press run – the number of copies printed in a single printing.
Running back:	A headline or chapter title repeated at the top of each page, giving the reader a quick reference.
Saddlestich:	A binding process that fastens the pages or signatures of a book together with wire stitches or staples through the middle fold.
Sans serif:	A style of typeface that does not have serifs or ticks at the ends of the letters.

Screen:	A network of crisscross lines of dots which break-up a continuous tone image into a pattern that can be printed in black and white to represent gradations of grey. Without a screen photographs will be reproduced as if by a copy machine. Used to make half-tones.
Self publisher:	Realistic and courageous author who understands the reality of the publishing market, knows that a book is a product, and takes control of his or her destiny.
Serifs:	Small extensions or "ticks" on the bases and tops of letters. They make the type easier to read because they lead the eye to the next letter.
Service bureau:	A company that specialises in support services for designers, printers and photographers. Service bureaus do screening halftones, colour separations, proofs and camera proof output.
Sheet fed press:	A printing press that prints on individual sheets of paper. Each sheet is then folded and trimmed to make a signature. Most economical for short-run books.
Shrink wrap:	A clear plastic covering, heat shrunk to fit tightly around quantities of books. Helps to protect books during shipping and from humidity. Sometimes enhances salability.
Signature:	A part of a book consisting of a group of pages that has been folded and trimmed. There may be 4,8,16,24 or 32 pages to a signature. The book should be planned so that the page count comes out in even signatures.
Smart self-publisher:	Someone who does it right.
Smyth sewn:	Signatures sewn together with thread by linked stitching on back of fold and through centerfold fold, permitting the binding to open almost flat, and strengthening the entire book block.
Spine:	The back of a bound book connecting two covers. Title, author's name, and sometimes publisher's imprint and/or ISBN are printed on it.
Stripping:	Placing the various elements of the layout on their respective positions on the flats which will be used to make the final plates.
Subsidy press:	A publishing company that applies its ISBN to a book and charges the author for the cost of production. The author receives only the copies of the book, and is promised royalties on those copies that might be sold by the subsidy press.
Tag:	In HTML, the code that will tell the browser software to apply, or to stop applying, a certain type or style of format to a part of a document.

Title page:	The page in a book's front matter, usually recto, which states the title, author, and publisher, following the half-title page.
Trade paperbacks:	The name given to the common soft cover books sold to bookstores. Usually they are 6in by 9in or 5.5in by 8.6in and are printed on substantial paper. For "mass market".
Trap:	An area of overlapping ink where different colours meet. Traps prevent unwanted white edges, where the colour shows through, between areas of different colours.
Typeface:	A style or design of type encompassing weight, shape and weight, and proportions which make it distinct from other typefaces. Use a conventional typeface for your body text.
Typo:	Another word for typographical error. Find them during the proofing process, not at blueline stage or after the book is in print.
UV coating:	A liquid protective coating applied to covers or dust jackets during the printing process that is dried out by ultraviolet light. Not as protective as film lamination but better than varnish.
Uncoated paper:	Paper on which the printing surface consists of the paper stock itself. Usually used to print the body of a book . Books made with uncoated cover stock (card stock) usually look home made.
Underlining:	Don't use it for titles or emphasis in books. Use italics.
URL:	Universal Resource Locator – the address of a site on the World Wide Web.
Vanity press:	Another term for subsidy press. It implies that the published book has no value other then to stroke the author's ego.
Varnish:	A thin protective coat applied to a printed sheet or cover during the printing process. It provides protection and gives gloss for appearance. Cheaper than lamination but with less gloss and providing less protection.
Verso:	A left hand page of a book, properly an even-numbered page The verso page contains the copyright and other important information.
Walk-around:	A person dressed in a costume. who walks round a mall or shopping centre during the booksigning to help promote a book.
Web:	See World Wide Web.
Webmaster:	A computer buff who is able to produce exceptionally striking art and format of pages on the World Wide Web.
Web press:	A printing press that uses large rolls of paper rather than individual sheets. Economical for long print runs (more

	than 10,000 copies). Newspapers and magazines are printed on web presses
Web page:	A page on the web site, usually the home page, but any page if the site has more than one page.
Wholesales:	A price given to resellers which reflects the discount from a stated retail price.
Widow:	A short single line at the top of a page or column, usually the last line of the last paragraph from the preceding page. To be avoided in good typesetting. Also, a single word or syllable produced by a bad break standing alone as the last line of a paragraph.
World Wide Web:	The network of personal and commercial information sites on host for individual Web sites which consist of home pages and other pages connected to home pages via hyperlinks.
Zee	Secret for success is to do the book right!

COMPUTER PRINTOUTS
AIDS TO PUBLISHING CONTRACTS
PRICES & PRINT-RUN DETERMINATIONS
Machinations in Coal Mining
& Book Publishing Experience Contracts

CONTRACTS ANALYSED
1 – Vanity Press Publisher:-
The first manuscript, publishing of which was undertaken by a member of the Vanity Press – fraternity – Direct identification has been deliberately avoided – in that the motivation for writing this book was neither by "emotion or anger" but more constructively as a vehicular "back-feed of informational experience and innovation" designed to eliminate or control nefarious and questionable practices perpetrated by a minima of un-scrupulous operators – I believe the publishing industry has little time for.

The more enlightened the "public" can become, of the situations prevailing and described the better its chances of dealing with that minima of un-representative operators in its own way.

I hope I have been able to make a contribution in that direction.

2 – In the case of the second manuscript the publishing of which has been accomplished somewhat in the manner of a "book packager" the contrasting experience in terms of pleasure, co-operation and enterprise has been truly remarkable.

COMPUTER PRINTOUTS
In the Chapter "Computer Aids To Forecasting" an introduction is made to the work I have done in the construction of "computer spreadsheet aids" with reference to the "validity" and "optimum values" of a publishers "capital, print run and retail book" price fixing relative to his contracts.

This is the point at which a publisher's irregularities in terms of "price fixing" may be challenged – before any commitment is made or damage arises. Knowing what constitutes the reasonable, and what is to be considered the highly irregular, places an author in a position of strength, which can be used to circumvent both damage and stress, that might otherwise develop.

Here with is an assortment of "computer spreadsheets" I have designed and worked with – they are reasonably easy to construct, in which case I would be glad to provide help or supply.

PRINTER (PACKAGER) QUOTATION

5 The Marina
Harbour Road
LYDNEY
Gloucestershire
GL15 5ET

Telephone:01594 843830
Fax:01594 842514
e-mail artytype.lydney@dial.pipex.com

BASIC VALUES QUOTED

CHOICE	CAPITAL	RUN	CAPITA
1	£4,700	1,000	£4.70
2	£5,000	1,500	£3.33
3	£5,300	2,000	£2.65
TOTALS	£15,000	4,500	£10.68

At this early stage the Publisher has great flexibility – but the Author is unaware of such situations . There has been no consultation , the cheaper "the per capita book price" the greater the flexibility re promotional & complimentary copy.

SPREADSHEET ANALYSIS.

PRINTOUT – 1. Choice 1 Here greater detail indicates what could be expected in the worst situation.

PRINTOUT – 2. Choice 2 Here is what average potential is to be accepted.

PRINTOUT – 3. Choice 3 Here is the best situation which can develop.

140

ANALYSIS:- PUBLISHER'S CAPITAL CONTRACT CONDITIONS   No.1

PRINT OUT 1A

	b	c	d	e	f	g	h	i	j	k	l	m	n
Capital	4700	Print Run	500	500	to	1000					0.81	950	1000
		Increment		50			Conversion Factor						

ELEMENT

ELEMENT			d	e	f	g	h	i	j	k	l	m	n
Range of Print Run	4		500	550	600	650	700	750	800	850	900	950	1000
	5												
	6												
	7		£9.40	£8.55	£7.83	£7.23	£6.71	£6.27	£5.88	£5.53	£5.22	£4.95	£4.70
Capital Cost Per Book	8												
Per Book Cost Breakeven	9	Lower	£11.59	£10.54	£29.33	£8.91	£8.28	£7.73	£7.24	£6.82	£6.44	£6.10	£5.79
	10			Profit Margin 0 to 100 Percent Breakeven Price									
Retail Book Price	11	*Upper	£23.18	£21.07	£58.66	£17.83	£16.56	£15.45	£14.49	£13.63	£12.88	£12.20	£11.59
	12												
Breakeven Minima Sales	13		203	223	80	264	284	304	324	345	365	385	405.56
	14		*Based Upon Upper Limit Value										

	b	c	
Direct Sales %	52.8	0.53	Script Values "Exclusively Subject to Change from Computer"
Indirect Sales	47.22	0.47	Keyboard Cells – b3,b15, b17.c3 and c4
Sales Discount %	40	0.60	Retail Price fixed at twice the breakeven Book Price to provide a wide margin
	18		for consideration.

You may alter the values of any one, two or combination or all variables depicted in "italics" from the keyboard in which case relevant new values to their revised variables will be automatically computed.
This is probably the most useful and versatile of the calculating tools developed hereto and will be helpful to an authors check of the likely effects of a publishers assessment, of capital, print run and book retail prices.

COMPUTER SPREADSHEET PROGRAMME NO.2 – PRINTOUT NUMBER ONE
Modified & Revised Programme – with Extended Flexibility in terms of Print Run, Print Run Interval, Per Capital
Book Price, Breakeven Price, Profit Margins & Profits.

*Yields Per Capita Book Price. Breakeven Price & Retail Book Price Run 0 to 1000 in Increments of 50 (variable).
Capital £47,00 chose (variable) Direct Sales 52.80 Percent (variable). Indirect Sales 47.22 percent (variable).*

ANALYSIS:- PUBLISHER'S CAPITAL CONTRACT CONDITIONS   No-2

PRINTOUT-1A

	b	c	d	e	f	g	h	i	j	k	l	m	n
Capital Charge	5000	Print Run	500	to		1500	Conversion Fact:0.81						
	4	Increment	100										
ELEMENT	5												
Range of Print Run	6		500	600	700	800	900	1000	1100	1200	1300	1400	1500
Capital Cost Per Book	7		£10.00	£8.33	£7.14	£6.25	£5.56	£5.00	£4.55	£4.17	£3.85	£3.57	£3.33
Per Book Cost Breakever	8												
	9	Lower	£12.33	£10.27	£29.33	£7.71	£6.85	£6.16	£5.60	£5.14	£4.74	£4.40	£4.11
	10				Profit Margin 0 to 100 Percent Breakeven Price								
Retail Book Price	11	*Upper	£24.66	£20.55	£58.66	£15.41	£13.70	£12.33	£11.21	£10.27	£9.48	£8.81	£8.22
	12												
Breakeven Minima Sales	13		203	243	85	324	365	406	446	487	527	568	608.34
	14												
Direct Sales %	52.8	0.53			Script Values "Exclusively Subject to Change from Computer								
Indirect Sales	47.22	0.47			Keyboard Cells - b3, b15, b17, c3 and c4								
Sales Discount %	40	0.60			Retail Price fixed at twice the breakeven Book Price to								
	18				provide a wide margin for profit margin considerations								

You may alter the values of any one, two or combination of all variables depicted in italics from the in which case relevant new values to their revised variables will be automatically coputed

This is probably the most useful & versatile of the calculating tool's developed hereto & will be helpful to an authors check of the likely effects of a publishers assessments, of capital, print run & book retail prices

ANALYSIS:- PUBLISHER'S CAPITAL CONTRACT CONDITIONS — No-3

PRINTOUT-1A	b	c	d	e	f	g	h	i	j	k	l	m	n
Capital Charge	5300	Print Run	1000		to	2000	Conversion Fact 0.81						
	4	Increment	100										
ELEMENT	5												
Range of Print Run	6		1000	1100	1200	1300	1400	1500	1600	1700	1800	1900	2000
	7												
Capital Cost Per Book	8		£5.30	£4.82	£4.42	£4.08	£3.79	£3.53	£3.31	£3.12	£2.94	£2.79	£2.65
Per Book Cost Breakever	9	Lower	£6.53	£5.94	£29.33	£5.03	£4.67	£4.36	£4.08	£3.84	£3.63	£3.44	£3.27
	10		Profit Margin 0 to 100 Percent Breakeven Price										
Retail Book Price	11	*Upper	£13.07	£11.88	£58.66	£10.05	£9.33	£8.71	£8.17	£7.69	£7.26	£6.88	£6.53
	12												
Breakeven Minima Sales	13		406	446	90	527	568	608	649	689	730	771	811.12
	14												
Direct Sales %	52.8	0.53			Script Values "Exclusively Subject to Change from Computer								
Indirect Sales	47.22	0.47			Keyboard Cells - b3, b15, b17, c3 and c4								
Sales Discount %	40	0.60			Retail Price fixed at twice the breakeven Book Price to								
	18				provide a wide margin for profit margin considerations								

You may alter the values of any one, two or combination of all variables depicted in italics from the in which case relevant new values to their revised variables will be automatically caputed

This is probably the most useful & versatile of the calculating tool's developed hereto & will be helpful to an authors check of the likely effects of a publishers assessments, of capital, print run & book retail prices

INTERPRETING THE COMPUTED VALUES

Looking at the mass of values – you are quite entitled to ask what do they all mean – and what is being attempted. Maybe if you are not mathematically orientated – you ordinarily would shy away from attempting to get an understanding. Please bear with me, it is important. Dealing with the last point first:-

1. What we are trying to do is to determine what the Publisher has set up for us – in his assessment of the contract values *(evidence has indicated he doesn't know himself, and where he has over-capitalised deliberately or otherwise prefers not to know.)* will those values – give rise to a "breakeven, profitable, or heavy loss situation." Have we been mis-led, conned or taken *"for a ride"* as expressed in the American vernacular.

2. What sort of "print run" in relation to a "practical retail book price" would appear to be the most appropriate to our individual circumstances?

Let me explain as simply as I can – Having fed in the known capital value and print run, (the latter in the form of an incremental range and indeed the "sales split (52.8 over a sample of 72 books sold) and discounts on indirect sales (usually taken around 40 per cent) – the appropriate values are computed and revealed on the computer screen to be printed out. These are shown in Printout's No.1 – No.2 & No.3.

Row 5   This indicates the print run range 500 to 1,000 at intervals of 50.

Row 7   Gives the appropriate levels of "per capita book price".

Row 9   Provides the detail of the Breakeven Price at the relative print run levels. This is the profit margin base.

Row 11   This is a ceiling fixed arbitrarily between which the "retail book price" relative to the print level is being considered. Here the margin is fixed at 100% – it could be as low as 40. Anything less – increases the subsidy on the Retailers Profit.

Row 13   Indicates the minimum number of books that need to be sold to breakeven.

After all this – what are my allocated values to my own project. They are the averages of the three choices – Capital – Fixed by Packager and accepted as reasonable – £5,000. Print Run 1500. Retail book price £7.99 per copy (this would indicate an apparent profit £7.99 – $4.16 = £3.83. – not so, subsidising the Retailers excess 40% discounts, the true profit is £0.63, insignificant so far the application of upwards of three years tense effort is concerned. More importantly the object throughout has to been help those would-be writers who follow us to deal with the irregularities and exploitations of the past, more effectively. Moreover when St Peter at the Golden Gates asks what do you think qualifies you to enter? – it would be nice to reply –

"I've tried throughout my life – like Tony Benn to Help and Love my Fellowment" – with acknowledgements to Leigh Hunt and his poem "About Ben Adhem", written many years past.

COMPUTER PRINTOUTS
AIDS TO PUBLISHING CONTRACTS
SALES & PROFITABILITY DETERMINATIONS

COMPUTER SPREADSHEETS 4-8
Potential Sales & Profitabilities

Here we have a simplified spreadsheet version, of the former one examined earlier, which analyses potential direct, indirect and total sales, and profitability performances, with respect to whatever elemental values are chosen and fed into the programme.

The format of this programme provides for the least used variable s to be set down the LH Side – these are the :"Direct and Discounted Sales Percentages" where known. In the absence of firm fact, they are assumed at 50 and 40 per cent respectively.

Box No.1 contains the "main variable inputs" to the computer, Box No.2 output in terms of Total Sales and Profitability.

Input – Box No.1

– feeding in £14,000 as Capital. 800 as Print Run and £18.00 as the Books Retail Price –

computes to, in:-

Output Box no.2

Total: Sales of £11,800 with a potential Loss of £2,400.

Extremely simple and instantaneous to operate – no maths to be applied. Rather than deal with the individual spreadsheet exclusively, let me summarise same in the following manner.

COMPUTER PRINT-OUT NO'S 1 TO 9

Spread Sheet No.	Box No.1 Input			Box No.2 Output	
	Capital	Print-Run	Book Price	Sales	Profits /Loss
4	£14,000	800	£18.00	£11,500-	–£2,400
5	£9,000	1000	£15.00	£12,000	£3,000
6	£5,000	1500	£7.99	£9,721	£4,721
7	£5,300	2,000	£7.99	£12,962	£7.661
8	£6,000	600	£10.83	£5,271	£-497

When viewing such profitabilities – they can be substantially wiped out, or drastically reduced or losses increased when the 40% discount cuts of the Retail Book Stores are taken into consideration.

Computer Spreadsheet No. 9

This is quite a composite example with a very wide range of application. Having provision for identifying 2nd and subsequent Edition performances.

CAPITAL CHARGE - PRINT RUN & RETAIL BOOK PRICE COMPUTATION NO 4
SPREADSHEET "BASIC-£'S" PROGRAM NUMBER - 1

COMPUTER PRINTOUT No.1	Values Variables	Direct Sales	Indirect Sales	Total Sales Costs	Total Production	Profit or Loss
U.K. FORMAT IN £'S STERLING						
VARIABLES		£'S	£'S	£'S	£	£
AUTHOR'S CAPITAL CHARGE £'S	14,000	7,200.00	4,320.00	11,520.00	14,000.00	-2,480.00
PRINT RUN - NUMBER OF BOOKS	800					
Books Capital Cost Price - £'s:-	17.50	*BASIC VALUES KEYED IN*				
Books Breakeven Cost:-	£21.88	*Box No 1*				
DISCOUNT PERCENTAGE - %:-	40.00 0.40		CAPITAL	£14,000		
DIRECT SALES PERCENTAGE. %	50.00 0.50		PRINT RUN	800		
Compensating factor	0.80		BOOK PRICE	£18.00		
Indirect Sales Percentage:-	50.00 0.50					
Direct Sales - Number of Books:-	400	*COMPUTED VALUES AT*				
Indirect Sales - Number of Books:-	400	*Box No 2*				
PRODUCTION COST/BOOK £'S:-		TOTAL SALES		£11,520		
BOOKS RETAIL COST PRICE - £'S	18.00	PROFIT/LOSS		-£2,480		
UK / USA RATES £1 = $x	1.62					
AUTHORS PROFIT PERCENTAGE	100.00 1	7,200.00	4,320.00	11,520.00	14,000.00	
Publishers Profit Percentage:-	0.00 0.00	£0.00	£0.00	11,520.00	£0.00	

COMPUTER SPREADSHEET PROGRAMME NO.3 – PRINTOUT NUMBER ONE

This is a simple computation of a Publishers Fixed Contract Values, Capital, Print Run, Retail Book Price input – "Push-button response" Authors "output" Total Sales & Profit

Publisher	Authors
Input – Capital £14,000 – Print Run – 800	Total Sales £11,520 potential
Retail Book Price £18.00	Profit/Loss £2,480

CAPITAL CHARGE - PRINT RUN & RETAIL BOOK PRICE COMPUTATION NO 5
SPREADSHEET "BASIC-£'S" PROGRAM NUMBER - 1

COMPUTER PRINTOUT No.1	Values Variables	Direct Sales	Indirect Sales	Total Sales	Total Production Costs	Profit or Loss
		£'S	£'S	£'S	£'S	£
U.K. FORMAT IN £'S STERLING						
VARIABLES						
AUTHOR'S CAPITAL CHARGE £'S	9,000	7,500.00	4,500.00	12,000.00	9,000.00	3,000.00
PRINT RUN - NUMBER OF BOOKS	1000					
Books Capital Cost Price - £'s:-	9.00					
Books Breakeven Cost:-	£11.25					
DISCOUNT SALES PERCENTAGE - %:-	40.00	0.40				
DIRECT SALES PERCENTAGE. %	50.00	0.50				
Compensating factor	0.80					
Indirect Sales Percentage:-	50.00	0.50				
Direct Sales - Number of Books:-	500					
Indirect Sales - Number of Books:-	500					
PRODUCTION COST/BOOK £'S:-						
BOOKS RETAIL COST PRICE - £'S	15.00					
UK / USA RATES £1 = $x	1.62					
AUTHORS PROFIT PERCENTAGE	100.00	1	7,2500.00	4,500.00	12,000.00	9,000.00
Publishers Profit Percentage:-	0.00	0.00	0.00	£0.00	0.00	0.00

BASIC VALUES KEYED IN

Box No 1

CAPITAL	£9,000
PRINT RUN	1000
BOOK PRICE	£15.00

COMPUTED VALUES OUT

Box No 2

TOTAL SALES	£12,000
PROFIT/LOSS	-£3,000

COMPUTER SPREADSHEET PROGRAMME NO.3 – PRINTOUT NUMBER ONE

This is a simple computation of a Publishers Fixed Contract Values. Capital, Print Run, Retail Book Price input – "Push-button response" Authors "output" Total Sales & Profit

Publisher	Authors	
Input – Capital £9,000 – Print Run – 1000	Total Sales	£12,000 potential
Retail Book Price £15.00	Profit/Loss	£3,000

CAPITAL CHARGE - PRINT RUN & RETAIL BOOK PRICE COMPUTATION NO 6
SPREADSHEET "BASIC-£'S" PROGRAM NUMBER - 1

COMPUTER PRINTOUT No.1	Values Variables	Direct Sales	Indirect Sales	Total Sales	Total Production Costs	Profit or Loss
						£
U.K. FORMAT IN £'S STERLING						4,721.27
VARIABLES		£'S	£'S	£'S	£'S	
AUTHOR'S CAPITAL CHARGE £'S	5,000	6,325.68	3,395.59	9,721.27	5,000.00	
PRINT RUN - NUMBER OF BOOKS	1500	*BASIC VALUES KEYED IN*				
Books Capital Cost Price - £'s:-	3.33	Box No 1				
Books Breakeven Cost:-	£4.11					
DISCOUNT SALES PERCENTAGE - %:-	0.40	CAPITAL		£5,000		
DIRECT SALES PERCENTAGE. %	0.53	PRINT RUN		1500		
Compensating factor	0.81	BOOK PRICE		£7.99		
Indirect Sales Percentage:-	0.53					
Direct Sales - Number of Books:-	792	*COMPUTED VALUES OUT*				
Indirect Sales - Number of Books:-	708	Box No 2				
PRODUCTION COST/BOOK £'S:-		TOTAL SALES		£9,721		
BOOKS RETAIL COST PRICE - £'S	7.99	PROFIT/LOSS		£4,721		
UK / USA RATES £1 = $x	1.62					
AUTHORS PROFIT PERCENTAGE	100.00	6,325.68	3,395.59	9,721.27	5,000.00	
Publishers Profit Percentage:-	0.00	£0.00	£0.00		0.00	

COMPUTER SPREADSHEET PROGRAMME NO.3 – PRINTOUT NUMBER THREE

Input – Capital £5,000 – Print Run – 1500   Output – Total Sales   £9,722 potential
Retail Book Price £7.99   Profit   £4,722

From the foregoing, and with this Particular programme, the Retail Book Price of this book was fixed at £7.99 – with a book sales split of 50% direct sales & a 40% discount on book retailers disposals, an Authors profit share thereon, (before deducting the value of complimentary, promotional, and statutory copy, and subsidising the retailer on the books total retail price (see page 126 – Example No.2), his profit could virtually be dissipated to about £945. In the event of debiting the cost of the complentary and promotional copy etc, be wiped out altogether in the form of total loss. There's more to price fixing than is shown on book covers.

CAPITAL CHARGE - PRINT RUN & RETAIL BOOK PRICE COMPUTATION NO 7
SPREADSHEET "BASIC-£'S" PROGRAM NUMBER - 1

COMPUTER PRINTOUT No.1	Values Variables	Direct Sales	Indirect Sales	Total Sales	Total Production Costs	Profit or Loss
U.K. FORMAT IN £'S STERLING						
VARIABLES		£'S	£'S	£'S	£'S	£
AUTHOR'S CAPITAL CHARGE £'S	5,300	8,434.24	4,527.45	12,961.70	5,300.00	7,661.70
PRINT RUN - NUMBER OF BOOKS	2000					
Books Capital Cost Price - £'s:-	2.65	*BASIC VALUES KEYED IN*				
Books Breakeven Cost:-	£3,27	*Box No 1*				
DISCOUNT SALES PERCENTAGE - %:-	40.00					
DIRECT SALES PERCENTAGE. %	52.78	CAPITAL		£5,300		
Compensating factor	0.81	PRINT RUN		2000		
Indirect Sales Percentage:-	47.22	BOOK PRICE		£7.99		
Direct Sales - Number of Books:-	1056					
Indirect Sales - Number of Books:-	944	*COMPUTED VALUES OUT*				
		Box No 2				
PRODUCTION COST/BOOK £'S:-						
BOOKS RETAIL COST PRICE - £'S	7.99	TOTAL SALES		£12,962		
		PROFIT/LOSS		£7,662		
UK / USA RATES £1 = $x	1.62					
AUTHORS PROFIT PERCENTAGE	100.00	8,434.24	4,527.45	12,961.70	5,300.00	
Publishers Profit Percentage:-	0.00	£0.00	£0.00	£0.00	0.00	

COMPUTER SPREADSHEET PROGRAMME NO.3 – PRINTOUT NUMBER FOUR

Input – Capital £5,000 – Print Run – 2000   Output – Total Sales   £12,962 potential
Retail Book Price £7.99   Profit   £7,662

This represents ARTYTYPE – the Printer's best offer – for an extra 500 books printed, but the sale of 500 "first edition – unknown writers" books are far more formidable than would seem to be the case, when browsing through a Retail Book Store.

149

CAPITAL CHARGE - PRINT RUN & RETAIL BOOK PRICE COMPUTATION   No.8
SPREADSHEET "BASIC-£'S" PROGRAM NUMBER - 1

COMPUTER PRINTOUT NO.1 U.K FORMAT IN £'S STIRLING	VALUES	VARIABLES	DIRECT SALES £'s	INDIRECT SALES £'s	TOTAL SALES £'s	TOTAL PRODUCTION COSTS £'S	PROFIT OR LOSS £
VARIABLES							
Authors Caoital Charge:-	6000		3,430	1,841	5,271	6,000	-£729.34
Print-run Number of Books	600						
Books Capital Cost Price - £'s:	£10.00		BASIC VALUES KEYED IN				
Books Breakeven Cost:-	£12.33	= 0.40	BOX No 1				
DISCOUNT SALES PERCENTAGE - %	40.00	0.53	CAPITAL		£6,000		
DIRECT SALES PERCENTAGE. %	52.78		PRINT-RUN		600		
Compensating factor.	**0.81**		BOOK PRICE		£10.83		
Indirect Sales Percentage :-	47.22	0.53	COMPUTED VALUES OUT				
Direct Sales - Number of Books:-	317		BOX NO 2				
Indirect Sales - Number of Books:-	283		TOTAL SALES		£5,271		
PRODUCTION COST PER BOOK £'S :-			PROFIT /LOSS		-£729		
BOOKS RETAIL COST PRICE - £'S	£10.83						
UK / USA EXCHANGE RATES £	1.62						
AUTHORS PROFIT PERCENTAGE:-	60.00	0.6	2,057.79	1,104.61	3,162.39	3,600.00	-£437.61
Publishers Profit Percentage:-	40.00	0.4	1,371.86	736.41	2,108.26	2,400.00	-£291.74

CAPITAL CHARGE – PRINT RUN & PER CAPITA BOOK PRICED – PROGRAMME 3. DETERMINATIONS

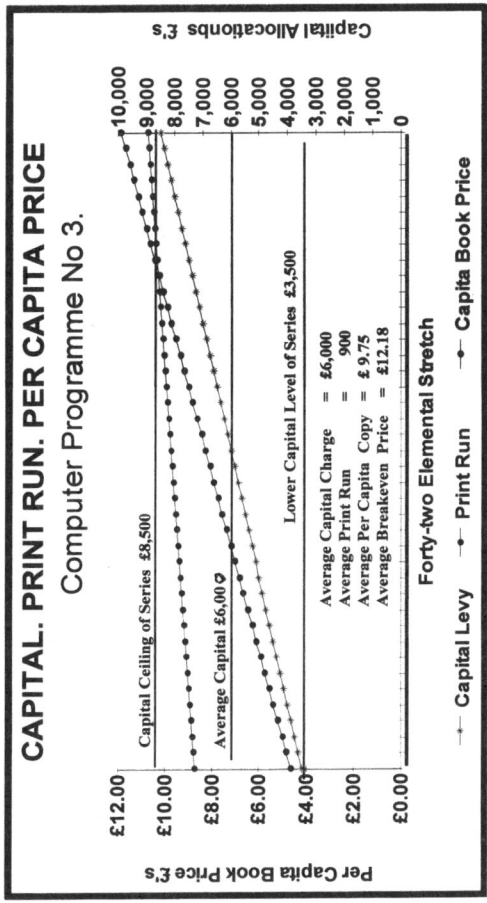

CAPITAL. PRINT RUN. PER CAPITA PRICE
Computer Programme No 3.

Per Capita Book Price £'s

Capital Ceiling of Series £8,500

Average Capital £6,000

Lower Capital Level of Series £3,500

Average Capital Charge	= £6,000
Average Print Run	= 900
Average Per Capita Copy	= £ 9.75
Average Breakeven Price	= £12.18

Forty-two Elemental Stretch

Capital Allocationbs £'s

—×— Capital Levy   —•— Print Run   —•— Capita Book Price

Incidentally the above I believe to be a far better guide than what is offered by the Publisher – Here the author is able to get some idea of the "Capital Levels " above the average of £6,000 quoted. When one compares a Capital of £14,000 as against the £8,500 as shown, there has to be something special, or the situation calls for deep analysis. relative to exploitation. Conceivably it might be used as a "litmus test" against what is being offered at any time.

COMPUTER PROGRAM NO.4

VARIABLES	Capital	Print	Per Capita Book	£-BOOK Price	SALES % DIRECT	Indirect Sales%	Factor Con'vsm	Retail Price	Product Costs Book	Total Costs 2nd Edit	Discount Percent
Publishers Minima Capital	£3,500	400									
INTERVAL INCREMENT	125	25	0.05	0.06	50.00	50.00	0.08	£8.75	£4.54	4,086	40.00
STARTING BASE:-	£3,500	400	8.75	10.94							

SERIES AVERAGE BOOKS:-£6,000.00   Average Print Run:- 900   Average Per Capital Book Cost:- £9.75

SERIES BREAK EVEN BOOK PRICE:- £12.19   Percentage Profit Margin 50   Retail Book Price £18.28

SERIES AVERAGES

RATIO=125/14.29=8.75	Levy On Author £	Print Run No.-	Per Capital £'s	Retail Price £	Direct Book No's	Indirect Book No's	Direct Sales £'s	Indirect Sales £	Total Sales £'s	Capital Recovery £'s	2nd Edit Profits £
RETAIL BOOK PRICE-£?											
MINIMUM LEVEL OF SERIES	3,500	400	£8.75	10.95	200	200	2188	1313	3500	-£2,500	-£586
	3,625	425	£8.80	11.00	213	213	2337	1402	3739	-£2,261	-£347
LOWEST CAPITAL REQUIRED	3,750	450	£8.85	11.05	225	225	2488	1493	3981	-£2,019	-£105
	3,875	475	£8.90	11.12	238	238	2640	1584	4225	-£1,775	£4,225
ALTHOUGH THE MINIMAL AND	4,000	500	£8.95	11.18	250	250	2794	1677	4471	-£1,529	£4,471
LOWER LEVELS OF CAPITAL	4,125	525	£9.00	11.24	263	263	2950	1770	4720	-£1,280	£4,720
ARE IDEN. AS QUOTED BY	4,250	550	£9.05	11.30	275	275	3107	1864	4971	-£1,029	£4,971
BY THE PUBLISHER	4,375	575	£9.10	11.36	288	288	3265	1959	5224	-£779	£5,224
	4,500	600	£9.15	11.42	300	300	3425	2055	5480	-£520	£5,480
	4,625	625	£9.20	11.48	313	313	3587	2051	5638	-£362	£5,538
	4,750	650	£9.25	11.54	325	325	3750	2250	6000	-£0	£6,000
	4,875	675	£9.30	11.60	338	338	3914	2348	6263	£263	£6,263
	5,000	700	£9.35	11.66	350	350	4080	2448	6528	£528	£6,528
	5,125	725	£9.40	11.72	363	363	4248	2549	6796	£796	£6,796
	5,250	750	£9.45	11.78	375	375	4417	2650	7076	£1,067	£6,796
	4,625	625	£9.20	11.48	313	313	3587	2051	5638	£362	£5,638
		650	£9.25	11.54	325	325	3750		6000	-£0	£6,000
	4,875	675	£9.30	11.60	338	338	3914	2348	6263	£263	£6,263
	5,000	700	£9.35	11.66	350	350	4080	2448	6528	£528	£6,528
	5,125	725	£9.40	11.72	363	363	4248	2549	6796	£796	£6,796
	5,250	750	£9.45	11.78	375	375	4417	2650	7067	£1,067	£6,796
	5,375	775	£9.50	11.84	388	388	4587	2752	7339	£1,339	£7,067

	5,500	800	£9.55	11.90	400	400	4759	2855	7614	£1,614	£7,339
	5,625	825	£9.60	11.96	413	413	4932	2959	7892	£1,892	£7,892
	5,750	850	£9,65	12.02	425	425	5107	3202	8310	£2,310	£8,310
	5,875	875	£9.70	12.08	438	438	5284	3170	8454	£2,454	£8,454
AVERAGE CAPITAL REQUIRED	6,000	900	£9.75	12.14	450	450	5462	3277	8739	£2,739	£8,739
	6,125	925	£9.80	12.20	463	463	5641	3385	9026	£3,026	£9,026
	6,250	950	£9.85	12.26	475	475	5822	3493	9316	£3,316	£9,316
	6,375	975	£9.90	12.32	488	488	6005	3603	9608	£3,608	£9,608
	6,500	1000	£9.95	12.38	500	500	6189	3713	9902	£3,902	£9,902
	6,625	1025	£10.00	12.44	513	513	6374	3825	10199	£4,199	£10,199
	6,750	1050	£10.50	12.50	525	525	6750	3937	1068	£4,686	£10,686
	6,875	1075	£10.10	12.56	538	538	6561	4050	10611	£4,611	£10,611
	7,000	1100	£10.15	12.62	550	550	6940	4146	11103	£5,103	£11,103
	7,125	1125	£10,20	12.68	563	563	7131	4279	11410	£5,410	£11,410
	7,250	1150	£10.25	12.74	575	575	7324	4394	11719	£5,719	£11,719
	7,375	1175	£10.30	12.80	588	588	7519	4511	12030	£6,030	£12,030
	7,500	1200	£10.35	12.86	600	600	7715	4629	12343	£6,343	£12,343
	7,625	1225	£10.40	12.92	613	613	7912	4747	12659	£6,659	£12,659
	7,750	1250	£10.45	12.98	625	625	8111	4867	12978	£6,978	£12,978
	7,875	1275	£10.50	13.40	638	638	8311	4987	13298	£7,298	£13,298
	8,000	1300	£10.55	13.10	650	650	8513	5108	13621	£7,621	£13,621
	8,125	1325	£10.60	13.16	663	663	8717	5230	13947	£7,947	£13,936
	8,250	1350	£10.65	13.22	675	675	8922	5353	14275	£8,275	£14,264
	8,375	1375	£10.70	13.28	688	688	9128	5477	14605	£8,605	£14,594
MAXIMUM CAPITAL OF SERIES	8,500	1400	£10.75	13.34	700	700	9336	5602	14938	£8,938	£14,927
GRAND TOTALS	245000	36900	£399.75	497.64							
AVERAGE VALUE OF ELEMENTS	6000	900	£9.75	12.14							

COMPUTER SPREADSHEET PROGRAMME NO.FOUR
PRINTOUT NUMBER ONE
Capital £ Variable–Increments £125 Print Run Variable Increment–25
Retail Book Price–Derived Increment £0.06
Starting Values–Capital–£3,000 Print Run–400 Retail Book Price–£10.94
Maximum Values–Capital–£8,500 Print Run–1400 Retail Book Price–£13.34
Mathematically Interelated "Optimum Values" Publisher's Rough Capital Guide

Index

Since the Publisher indicates his minimum Capital Charge to be about £3,500 and his average Capital Investment £6,000 (See Executive Directors Statement of Policy Pages 30-31) I would estimate his "average print run" to be about 550 if there is any standard form, or mathematical pattern in his "contract price" fixing. Any substantial variation therefrom I believe would reflect "ad hoc" price assessments. With "Ad Hoc" price fixing for purposes best known to the Publisher himself, the true value of Print Run can only be determined by a detailed analysis of the actual total contracts involved.